DISCOVERING
LEADERS
within

DISCOVERING LEADERS *within*

A Modern Guide for Cultivating Your Team's Potential

L. Brett Larson

ISBN: 979-8-9850581-0-9 (trade paperback)
ISBN: 979-8-9850581-2-3 (ebook)

For bulk orders, signed copies, classes on emotional intelligence, interest in speaking engagements or in bringing HUM-B-LE to your team, email brett@humessence.com.

Cover designer: Self-Publishing School
Editor: Margaret A. Harrell, margaretharrell.com
Illustrations: Kara Koenitzer Tate

Independently published by Brett Larson

To all the people I have led who helped me learn how to be a better Leader. I'm infinitely grateful for the discomfort, the emotional pain, and the sleepless nights that forced me to look in the mirror. The book is also dedicated to my three sons—Kyle, Keenan, and Cam—who, through their own development, confronted me with the challenge of being a better parent. Finally, to my wife Kara, for the consciousness she elevates in me with her unique perspective and loving challenge when I am not sufficiently self-aware. She observes subtle opportunities for growth that only someone close to me can see.

As you read *Discovering Leaders Within* you might want to take notes on key concepts or document something you want to implement in your team. To facilitate this, I have created an accompanying workbook. The workbook also includes famous quotes where they fit the chapter topic. **Scan** on the QR code below to receive your free copy.

CONTENTS

Introduction xi

Section 1: The Development of Great Teams—Leader Humility, Employee Engagement, Psychological Safety, and Followership 1

Chapter 1:   Humility: The Cornerstone of Great Leaders.... 3

Chapter 2:   Growing Employee Engagement 9

Chapter 3:   Fostering a Psychologically Safe Environment . 18

Chapter 4:   Creating Followership 32

Section 2: Growing Great Leaders 41

Chapter 5:   A New Approach to Leadership Development 46

Chapter 6:   The Case for Emotional Intelligence 50

Chapter 7:   HUMan-Based LEadership Development (HUM-B-LE) 54

Chapter 8:   The HUM-B-LE Methodology 61

Chapter 9:   Step 1—Measuring the Initial State 65

Chapter 10:   Step 2—Designing the LD Plan 71

Chapter 11:   Step 3—Developing Individual and Team Emotional Intelligence 76

Chapter 12:   Step 4—Addressing Custom Team Needs 93

Chapter 13:   Step 5—Implementing the Development Planning Process (DPP) 97

Chapter 14:   Step 6—Creating a Sustainment Plan 111

Chapter 15:   Step 7—Measure Future State 117

Chapter 16:   Wrapping it Up 122

Epilogue/Conclusion 125

Acknowledgments 127

Appendix 1: A Deeper Dive into Characteristics
    of Traditional Leadership Development Programs 129

Appendix 2: Helpful Lists 135

Appendix 3: QR Code for More Information on
    the HUM-B-LE program and LD Services
    Offered by Humessence, LLC 139

Bibliography 141

About the Author 149

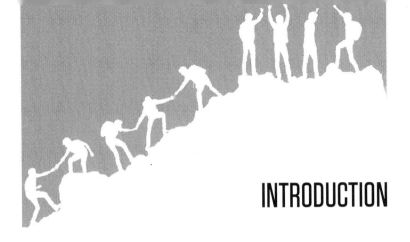

INTRODUCTION

My First Leadership Experience

We reap rich learning from our mistakes, and I've made my fair share. I'll never forget my first Leadership assignment, at twenty-five, which I vowed never to repeat.

The year was 1990. Four years into a career as an industrial engineer, I was growing restless. My job was to go into a manufacturing area—working with teams whose priority was just getting a product out—and implement quality-improvement projects. Having only mixed results to show for my struggles, it was at that point I decided instead of just trying to sell teams on the value of implementing a continuous-improvement program, I'd rather lead my own team and implement it myself. So, I applied and was selected as the next die-casting department supervisor. I did not realize yet that without any Leadership experience or training, I was a fish out of water.

At this point, a quick description of die casting would be helpful . . . Our die-casting processes were largely automated *and decidedly technical.* The process begins with a machine ladling molten aluminum from a furnace and pouring it into a steel sleeve. At high speed and pressure, the machine's plunger then pushes the molten aluminum into a mold cavity. In the cavity, the aluminum solidifies and the machine opens the mold, enabling another machine to pick the "shot" and place it on a conveyer belt. On the belt, the shot gets cooled while being transported to a manufacturing operator who places it on a trim press. The press trims the runners away from the part, which the operator then inspects, saving the good castings.

The operator is tasked with physically setting up all the equipment, downloading the settings electronically, and ensuring the system is producing good parts. Then the operator runs the process, filling out paperwork and keeping parts, which get sent on to subsequent processes. It is a dirty, hot, and potentially dangerous environment.

Our department was multi-shift, working around the clock, and it was a challenge to consistently produce high-quality castings. While I knew very little technically, I was inspired to learn and help improve the reliability of the operation. It was in this environment, *without any management training*, that I embarked on my first supervisory experience.

Operators, though highly skilled, generally lacked theoretical knowledge, which was masked by their practical experience. The best of them, however, through trial and error, had become experts in learning how to make good castings. Yet because their experiences varied, so did their approach to making good parts. And the next shift operator often changed the machine settings of the prior shift operator, who had a different approach. Multiplying the natural variation in the process, this created inefficiencies.

With no dedicated engineers supporting the department, my focus was to immerse myself in the theory; so I took numerous classes, read technical literature, listened to the technical representatives of the equipment manufacturers, and occasionally got my hands dirty learning from the operators about how to run the machines. While I included the most experienced operators in helping evaluate equipment options, I only minimally engaged them in studying process fundamentals with me. In retrospect, I treated them like they weren't capable of learning. My core belief—that I wasn't even conscious of yet—was that *operators were practicing art where science was needed.* In a word, I felt and acted *superior.*

While this was going on, ironically, I had the misplaced self-image that I cared about and respected each person. I was deeply lacking in emotional intelligence. And *a self-image that isn't aligned with behavior creates a learning opportunity, as I was about to find out.*

In an effort to assuage frustrations and keep unions away, my company encouraged employees to submit regular anonymous questions. All managers reviewed them every quarter. This was our management "council" process. After review, unless they were too offensive, the questions were read in front of an assembly of leaders. Following light discussion, a rough response would be composed that was eventually edited and posted throughout the company.

The first council meeting after I became a manager was not particularly noteworthy, but as time wore on, I became the target of an increasing number of questions/statements of irritation. These questions in no uncertain terms criticized me and the changes within the department. As months passed, the quantity of questions increased from one to several to many. And they began to get increasingly personal about me, employing phrases like, "wet behind the ears college boy."

I was getting absolutely torched in council and dreaded attending, even hoping I'd catch a cold or find some other convincing excuse to miss. With every question that was read, I could feel my peers glancing over, wondering what I'd done this time to invoke criticism. As I sat there listening, I pondered: *Why on earth is everyone ganging up on me? Can't they see I'm just trying to do the right thing? I just want to make our processes better!*

My boss, the Operations Leader, reassured me that it was just resistance to change, probably downplaying the situation too much. Regardless, when the council rolled around, my team's exasperation was there on paper for everyone to see. It was about six months into my new role when I realized the significant load of stress I was carrying. This prompted me to buy a heavy punching bag, which I hung in my basement at home. A couple of times a week, more frequently during council week, I went downstairs and punched the bag as hard and fast as I could to relieve stress. I think, given the alarming discomfort of the situation, I was metaphorically trying to "punch my way out."

About nine months into my supervisory role, spring rolled around. *Why not do something to try to connect with my team and build comradery?* A department picnic might be just what we needed. What better activity than to be paid to eat, throw horseshoes, and play volleyball together? This was going to be the start of a healthier relationship with my team!

First, I created a sign-up sheet and asked the team to fill in their names when they got a chance. This was going to be great! Any frustrations with my approach would dissolve away as we ate and played together. My spirits were high.

After several days passed, I checked in on the sign-up sheet. *No one had signed up.* Not one. Well, wasn't it to be expected? They were busy and probably hadn't gotten around to it. I just needed to remind them, and that's what I did.

Another couple of days passed. At last, one name appeared on the list. As I walked toward the sheet, wondering which brave soul signed up first, I hoped that this would open the floodgates. Standing in front of the sheet, I read the name. It wasn't even familiar to me. Was there someone in the department I hadn't met? Who was this person? I stood

Potluck Sign Up Sheet

Name	Dish / Item
1. CRAVEN R. SPECT	
2.	
3.	
4.	
5.	
6.	
7.	

there, pondering, before it hit me. The "volunteer" was just a fictional character! I could almost feel the operators behind me, watching with disdain as I decoded the name: "Craven R. Spect."

So *"Craving Respect" was how I made my team feel?!* Tail between my legs, I walked back to the office, asking myself where I had failed. *I cared about people! Didn't I? I treated them well, right? I was trying to help our department be successful; didn't they know that!* Still reeling from the revelation that I was deeply unpopular with my team, wounded in my self-image, I slept restlessly that night.

The next day, an operator came into my office with a question about production priorities. As I started to answer automatically, like always, it struck me. This person most likely knew the answer and probably just wanted reassurance. I remember thinking: *Holy shit, I've created an environment where the employees don't feel safe making basic, independent decisions. This isn't right.* For the first time, I realized that my drive to improve had undercut individual autonomy. That moment was a chance to establish a new relationship. So, I responded, "What do *you* think?"

Thus began the long journey to redefine my relationship with my team. It started with an innocuous little event that sparked a moment of self-awareness made possible because I was soul-searching for how to be a better Leader.

Where my behavior had demonstrated that I felt like a know-it-all and was overly controlling, I now endeavored to listen and learn much more than I talked and taught. Craven became my teacher, and through the temporary pain of this experience I realized that to be a Leader, I needed to humble myself. I needed to see my team as skilled individuals—to learn their depth of practical knowledge and value their years of experience. Before I could hope to gain their trust or have any ability to influence them, I needed to learn from them and be respectful of what they had to offer.

As I look back, it was not the technical skills of leading that were my deficit. I could assess problems, create a strategy, manage projects, understand manufacturing processes and flow, make a financial case for improvements, communicate ideas, and so on. Yes, I still had gaps, but none of this mattered because I lacked the soft skills of self-awareness and the ability to relate to my team. I lacked an ability to connect, to appreciate, to unite, to motivate. I believe that the magnitude of the pain often determines the depth of the learning. This deeply painful nine months taught me more about Leadership than any Leadership Development (LD) program could have; it is where

> . . . to be an effective Leader, I needed to humble myself.

I first realized the foundational importance of both emotional intelligence and humility.

Simplified Leadership Philosophy

Thirty years and numerous mistakes later, I've taken this painful experience as a motivator. I now see Leadership, simply, as having two primary responsibilities:

1. To translate organizational strategy into local team objectives, goals, and priorities
2. To create an environment and culture that enables <u>team</u> success

When a Leader ensures the team is aligned with broad objectives, it focuses and unites its efforts. The second primary objective a Leader has is service to the team's needs—attending to them and breaking down barriers to their success. This approach has supremely rewarded me personally. Ultimately, it led to the realization that the most fulfilling part of my role as a Leader was in helping people grow, which, in turn, led to my eventual focus on Leadership Development as a career.

Why this book is written for you

At first glance, you might consider this book to be narrowly applicable—for existing Leaders looking to improve their craft, or possibly for Leadership Development (LD) professionals interested in learning new approaches for growing Leaders. *Discovering Leaders Within* also, obviously, targets senior executives curious about improving the capability of Leaders in their organization. To address a targeted need for growing Leaders, I would point your focus to Part 1 of the book.

While all this is true, the need for being emotionally aware is universal. How does it relate to you and your job? The principles of the above example where I "messed up" in my short-sightedness are no different than when anyone starts an unknown project or, for that matter, creates a new relationship; it takes time, and things will go south at some point. If it's important, you just need to commit to working through the rough parts and be candid about your learning process. In sum, a broad pool of people can greatly benefit from reading this book. It has equal and specific utility in improving everyday human interactions.

Now a daily pursuit of mine is to stay aware, learn from others, and reflect on my thoughts and emotions, which always have something to teach me. Below are a few examples of broader questions that this book enlightens—where it can routinely benefit us in and outside of work:

- What is Emotional Intelligence (E.I.), and why is it so important for creating healthy relationships and general satisfaction in my life?

- What are some practices I can adopt to help me grow my emotional intelligence?

- How can I improve even my difficult relationships?

- How can I more effectively give and receive sensitive feedback?

- Why is humility so important in Leading and influencing others?

- How does my attitude affect my ability to engage others? What can I do about it?

- How can I create an environment of "collaborators," where my team at work or my family at home feels respected and are comfortable being authentic?

Capitalization of "L" in Leader

I capitalize the word "Leader" to distinguish a courageous, emotionally intelligent, team-empowering, service-oriented capital "L" Leader from a small "l" leader, who lacks humility, followership, and selflessness. In the initial story of this book, I was a small "l" leader. Small "l" leaders are not self-aware, do not sufficiently value the capabilities of their team, and often neglect the importance of relationships. They tend to overly depend on the power of their position. A capital "L" Leader, by contrast, has stable values that don't fluctuate or disappear under stress. In this Leader's team everyone is significant; each person contributes individual strengths and passions that are key to success. And these Leaders have conviction; they have the courage to challenge their own superiors. And they value influence over authority. A Leader is the first to fight injustice, the last to take credit.

> A Leader has stable values that don't fluctuate or fade when challenges arise.

A title doesn't make a Leader, and it may be hard to describe a great Leader, but it's easy to recognize one by *your* desire to follow that person. This type of Leader is what we aim to develop in *Discovering Leaders Within*. It's also someone who most closely resembles the archetype of a Servant Leader.

While hundreds of terrific books on Leadership have supported my personal development over the years, I don't recall reading much of anything related to how to create a successful LD program that is *both* practical and financially effective. Thus, outlining the importance of being a Servant Leader and sharing a process for creating them is the purpose of this book.

Organization of this Book

Part 1 focuses on key mechanics in creating and empowering a high-performing team. It starts with an appreciation of the power of humility in a Leader. Then I detail proven approaches that create engaged employees, an environment of psychological safety, and strong Leader followership. These principles apply equally well to creating a close-knit family, or church fellowship, or community. Skilled Leaders can create healthy teams in any environment when they build engagement, psychological safety and serve the needs of those they lead.

Part 2 introduces a program that I call HUMan-Based LEadership (HUM-B-LE). As the basis for building healthy relationships, it places foundational importance on teaching emotional intelligence. In Part 2 you learn the steps involved in the HUM-B-LE methodology and how they create a system that grows high-performing Servant Leaders.

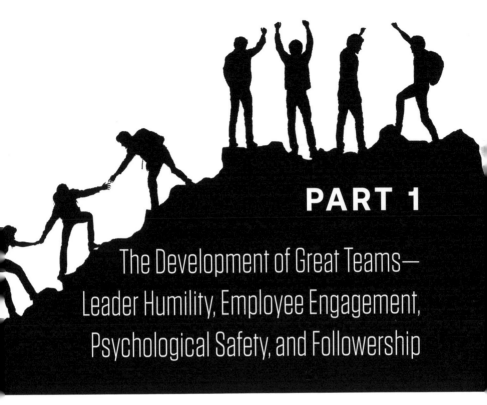

PART 1

The Development of Great Teams— Leader Humility, Employee Engagement, Psychological Safety, and Followership

A single Leader can apply this material to create a high-performing team. The insights shared in this section also help create a satisfying life with fulfilling relationships.

Humility: When Leaders conduct themselves with humility, it creates space for each person to contribute their unique skills, perspectives, and ideas. Humility says, *I don't have all the answers. I invite others' participation in determining the best path forward.* But do not confuse humility with weakness. It is not indecisive and does not mean you back away from problems or interpersonal challenges. It means you address these with curiosity and openness. But also decisiveness after weighing all factors. The difference is that humble Leaders take the time to understand and explain the why's behind decisions and don't just hide behind their authority. Humble Leaders live by the Socratic quote: "The only true wisdom is in knowing that you know nothing."

Engagement: Employee engagement correlates with superior business results, according to the Gallup State of the Global Workplace Report (representing "the collective voice of the global employee") and similar studies. In *Discovering Leaders Within,* I simply leverage their conclusions and apply the questions they defined to assess engagement. I don't relitigate the value of engagement, but I do share a process for growing it.

Psychological Safety (PS): PS is a shared belief that team members feel safe to be themselves; they won't be embarrassed, rejected, or punished for speaking up. They feel comfortable airing their perspectives and challenging current practices. With the seminal work of Amy Edmondson (professor of Leadership and Management at the Harvard Business School) on psychological safety and the key findings in a multiyear study by Google, code-named "Project Aristotle," PS has been identified as a key ingredient for high-performing teams. While this concept is of critical importance, there's limited practical guidance on how to create the environment. In this section, I detail an effective process for seeding, encouraging, creating, and maintaining PS.

Followership: Great Leaders aren't a cumulative list of competencies; they're great Leaders when they have influence and they create willing followers. So, how do you develop strong followership? In Part 1 of this book, I share a process for measuring it, the application of which will grow it.

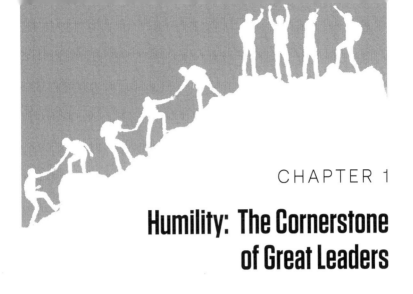

Humility: The Cornerstone of Great Leaders

*T*ed *Lasso*, an Apple TV show, stars a fictional Division II football coach who gets hired to coach a British Premier League soccer team and achieves success with minimal knowledge of the sport. This unlikely situation stemmed from the recently divorced team owner, Rebecca, wanting to get back at her cheating ex-husband. For retribution, she sought to cause his prized team to fail.

Though he lacks any relevant soccer experience, Rebecca hires Ted to coach her AFC Richmond team. Ted is unaware of her motives or how to teach the sport. But he knows people, how to coach, and is relentlessly positive while displaying high E.I.

Witnessing Ted's infectious good humor, immunity from ridicule, and ability to connect with players, the TV viewers begin to glimpse hope in the team's long-term potential for success. We are riveted by his ability to solve interpersonal problems and win over others through kindness, directness, and a talent for analogy.

While imaginary, the success of Ted as a coach seems plausible. He prioritizes developing relationships—with the owner, the team staff, the players, the press, and even those he meets in the community. He creates an atmosphere of camaraderie. He receives feedback thoughtfully and fosters discussion. He empowers the experts in the game, even if they previously resigned themselves to unassuming roles, such as the team water boy Nate. Through encouragement and respect for his unique talents, Lasso is able to bring out Nate's depth of knowledge, powers of observation, and knack for soccer strategy. What motivates each player? Ted finds out, and he understands that his ability to connect in the locker room will determine individual growth and the team's success.

Also, in uncomfortable instances of interpersonal team conflict, Ted Lasso calmly faces the uproar. At one point, a player disagrees with a decision he assumed Ted made, confronts him in front of the team, then walks off the field. Lasso follows him off the field to ask what's bothering him. After listening, he shares the truth of the matter, explaining that what was assumed hadn't actually happened. At the end of the conversation, Lasso calmly says, "You realize I'm going to have to have you run laps?" The player responds, "I wish you would."

Ted Lasso is a fantastic Servant Leader, who greatly exemplifies humility and high E.I. He makes the viewer believe that anything is possible when Leaders suspend their ego, develop relationships, and are resolutely focused on cultivating the best that everyone has to offer.

Books and papers detail the value of humility in a Leader, with possibly the best being *Good to Great* by Stanford professor Jim Collins. Deeply researching the topic, Collins revealed that at the helm in organizations with the highest long-term financial performance are "Level 5 Leaders." What these Leaders had in common was a unique blend of humility and a drive—above and beyond their personal interests—to execute the organization's mission. Even if uncomfortable, even if it required them to take personal risks, they drove organizational objectives. Their forte wasn't intelligence, experience, strategic thinking, an ability to inspire, or any other traditionally accepted attribute of a great Leader. At the core was humility. Humility sets these high-performing Leaders apart and is why reinforcing it is an objective of the HUM-B-LE development method.

Humility is a powerful source of Leader success for multiple reasons:

1. Humility makes space for **participation.** Humble Leaders are likely to speak last. They create space for their team to participate.

2. Humility creates **psychological safety (PS)**. With PS, team members know they won't be embarrassed, rejected, or punished for speaking up. They overcome their natural trepidation to offer ideas and risk being wrong or sounding stupid. Humility insists, "It's safe to be your true self."

3. Humility creates **inclusion**. While this is similar to psychological safety, where people are motivated to participate, inclusion adds a sense of belonging to a team united by purpose. When the Leader is humble, team members welcome the contribution of every other team member, knowing that each has an important perspective to share.

4. Humility raises company and societal objectives above personal interests. This allows the consistent application of **company values** undiluted by

personal interests. Without humility, the next crisis has leaders centralizing control. With humility, Leaders continue to apply organizational values and demonstrate confidence in the employees. This consistency enables dispersed authority, which creates speed, flexibility, and decisiveness.

5. Humility creates **trust**. A consistent, empowering, values-based Leader is a trustworthy Leader. Trust builds loyalty. It also drives business efficiency. As # 1 *New York Times* and *Wall Street Journal* bestselling author Stephen M. R. Covey so effectively illustrated in his book, *The Speed of Trust: The One Thing That Changes Everything*, **high trust is always faster and cheaper.**

Humility in Practice

One of the exciting things about writing this book is that integrity requires that I walk the talk. As such, I'm reminded to practice humility myself—to be conscious of my humility when engaging with Leaders and trying to help students discover personal insights. For example, when I work with a team, I partner with the senior Leader and ask that person to take a role in delivering content.

I've found that this impacts the Leaders threefold. First, by learning the material at a deeper level. Second, integrity encourages them to embody the concepts they teach. And finally,

as the senior Leader demonstrates personal growth, it motivates the team to engage more deeply. The salient point is that the act of teaching any philosophy motivates the teacher to embody the philosophy. This is why, in deploying the HUM-B-LE approach, we make the extra effort to partner with Leaders.

The HUM-B-LE development process places relationships at the center of the Leader's priorities. It's people who execute the mission of a company. It's people who interact with and create the experience of the customer. And it's Leaders who are tasked with building the positive, purposeful relationships that enable the positive execution of business operations. Humility as a catalyst makes this possible.

Deliverable:

This chapter establishes the foundational importance of humility for a Leader. Humility has a multiplier effect in creating participation, psychological safety, inclusion, trust, and alignment with company values.

Chapter 1 Summary:

- Humility in a Leader is a powerful paradigm that enables **participation, psychological safety, inclusion, leveraging of company values, and trust.**

- A Leader's humility enables the team to perform and achieve **superior business results.**

Practice:

This week, at the end of each day, paying special attention to any challenging interactions, take ten minutes to reflect on your day. Review what happened. How did you participate? What's the message for you, and how could you have approached conversations better; what will you do differently next time? As you reflect, be aware whether you're judging yourself or others, as bad. Judgment creates a barrier to learning; so, give up the judgment and focus on the learning.

Growing Employee Engagement

To measure team member engagement, we use the eight statements below that are rooted in Gallup's research and further refined by Marcus Buckingham and Ashley Goodall in *Nine Lies About Work*:

1. I am really enthusiastic about the mission of my company.
2. At work, I clearly understand what is expected of me.
3. In my team, I am surrounded by people who share my values.
4. I have the chance to use my strengths every day at work.
5. My teammates have my back.
6. I know I will be recognized for excellent work.
7. I have great confidence in my company's future.
8. In my work, I am always challenged to grow.

Buckingham and Goodall detail the importance of each statement. We apply their findings as a method for assessing team effectiveness, identifying areas of opportunity, and measuring the success of our LD program in driving improvement.

Recently I was coaching a very self-critical Leader named Christian, who was venting his frustration at not being able to get control of a couple of professional and personal issues. It felt to me like his self-criticism was blocking him from being freed up to identify options. So, I asked Christian, "What experience have you had as a Leader that you're most proud of?"

He paused for a moment; then I could see a warmth come over him as he dived into this story. Several years back, he said, he asked his team to write what they appreciated about each other, and where they would like to see each improve. After gathering up all the notes, Christian wrote each team member a summary of all the good things their teammates had said about them—on purpose disregarding the negatives. He distributed the gratitude summaries out to each person in the form of a Christmas card.

Then Christian got choked up as he recalled the wonderful impact of this act, as teammates shared what a great emotional boost it gave them at the time. Recently, ten years after he distributed these cards, he ran into one of these teammates he hadn't seen for years. In that short encounter, the person remembered receiving that card and thanked Christian again. It was one of the best things they had ever experienced at work, both concluded; his card, the teammate said, had driven him to commit to making a positive impact every day. In short, it had motivated him to increase his effort and overall performance as it was the first time he really felt valued.

Christian brightened with the recollection. He remembered how he hadn't thought it was a big deal until his team expressed their gratitude and stepped up their commitment. This recollection reminded him that he impacts people more than he knows. This simple reflection helped relieve some of Christian's self-imposed stress. It revitalized his sense of purpose and gently nudged him to not be so self-critical. Ultimately, this reminder renewed his hope, helping him get through his temporary challenges.

This story is emblematic of some of the nuances that exist. When a Leader purposefully notices the good (Question 6), it helps people believe their contributions are important, and it increases their engagement and contributions to the organization. Here are some additional nuggets that the engagement assessment in the list of "lies" above reveal:

1. Leaders must spend time developing relationships with those they lead. To create the feeling that someone has their back, a certain level of intimacy is necessary. Developing relationships also enables the Leader to know enough about the employee to utilize their strengths daily.

2. Engagement isn't just a contest in niceness. It also requires honest, respectful conversations to generate clarity: "I clearly understand what is expected of me."

3. Recognition for good work is critical. So often, people become Leaders because they have a critical eye; they are perfectionists. Engagement requires Leaders to move beyond a focus on flaws, to recognizing and expressing sincere appreciation for the positive.

4. A basis in shared values creates a consistency of priority. Emphasizing clarity of values enables employees to make decisions confidently. Knowing they have shared, defined values means employees don't have to guess at what's important to consider

when making decisions. And consistency demands organizational integrity; i.e., that corporate actions align with the company's stated values.

Let's now reflect on how values-based relationships inspire us to contribute our time and energy *because we are a part of something.* This contrasts with transactional relationships—a tit-for-tat approach of, "If you complete this project, I'll pay you a bonus." Transactional thinking is limiting and creates a "What's in it for me?" attitude. Values-based thinking is about doing something because it's the right thing to do. This broadens our perspective, as we start considering what's good for the team and/or organization, not just what's good for me. Connecting with common values is expansive and enables achievement of the highest potential.

In one episode of the *Hidden Brain* podcast, a daycare center was experiencing a low rate of parents being late to pick up their kids. The center wanted to eliminate this behavior, though it was infrequent. They decided to introduce a late fee for parents to pay when they arrived ten or more minutes late.

> When relationships become transactional, true ownership is lost and a what's-in-it-for-me attitude prevails.

The product of this policy change was that the fee had actually created a significant **increase** in lateness. Previously, parents had behaved responsibly because it was the right thing to do and out of valuing the time of the childcare professionals. When the fee was introduced, the relationship became transactional, causing parents to shed value-based thinking and loyalty. Instead, they considered their lateness acceptable because they were exchanging it for a fee. The value of timeliness and respect was replaced by transactional thinking: paying for the privilege of being late.

After seeing the effect of the fee on parental behavior, the daycare center reversed its policy to try to return to the previous lower rate of tardiness. Unfortunately, eliminating the late fee didn't resurrect value-based thinking. Transactional thinking had already been adopted, and it wasn't easily reversed. Lateness persisted.

The moral of this story is that Leaders and organizations should focus on value alignment to create engagement. When relationships become transactional, true ownership is lost and a sense of connection eroded. A "What's in it for me?" attitude prevails. One clear example of this, in my experience, is with attendance. Expecting people to be reliable because the team counts on each other and it's important to achieving team objectives is values-based thinking. When lawyers stepped in to say that Leaders couldn't give feedback about reliability and commitment to the team and our only recourse was to give written warnings once vacation time had been consumed, the relationship became transactional. This created a culture where all employees used up their paid sick leave. Sick time went from being a safety net to something that needed to be consumed, and overall attendance dropped.

The treatment of sick leave can be a challenging issue, with potential legal implications. So, it's not easily solved, but this example illustrates the importance for Leaders to understand the positive impact of values-based thinking. Leaders must consider how to promote it and minimize the influence of transactional thinking. Engagement is potentially at stake.

Finally, in my attempt to be a Servant Leader there is something I've done that has been surprisingly effective in creating engagement. In a staff meeting, I ask my team to identify their primary barriers to success. Generally, their responses will fall into four buckets:

- Issues outside of both their and my control (example: inefficient software systems)
- Issues outside of their control but that I can drive improvement in (example: sufficient resources for our team)
- Issues inside their control (example: a challenging relationship with a coworker)
- Issues that are just challenges that need to be worked through (example: the complexity of a project)

With this list identified, I commit to tackling the challenges one at a time, helping in three ways:

1. I will communicate issues outside of our control to the people who are able to address the challenge.
2. I will start, one at a time, working on issues in my control but outside of the team's control and provide updates.
3. I offer my support to the last two categories of issues: inside their control and ones that just need to be worked through.

As I utilize this process, those I lead see that I care, that I'm dedicated to their success. At the very least, they appreciate that, to me, they matter. They are also more motivated, as they see I am not just sitting on the sideline. And this conversation helps us unite on the challenges that hold our team back, building unity and embedding our shared responsibility—which results in increased engagement.

So how does this chapter on creating engagement apply more broadly to life? The role of parenting is one prominent example where this philosophy creates value.

All too often as a parent, when my sons made mistakes, I responded reflexively with anger and a lecture. When they broke an object, tried to sneak something past me, or talked back, losing my temper took attention off the act and put it *on me* and my reaction. The event became more about how *Dad was a jerk because he yelled at me.* No matter how justified I was, how I dealt with the situation determined whether my sons were simply victims of Dad's reaction or, on the other hand, clear-eyed about their behavior and able to take on personal responsibility.

While important, it was insufficient to have a thoughtful, engaging relationship with my sons and to notice their positive actions. Getting mad and yelling at them when something went wrong quickly wipes away this groundwork. But when I instead responded to their "bad" behavior by calmly talking about shared values (i.e. "Why is it important that we admit when we break something?"), it engages their minds in problem-solving together. I might then ask how their behavior may have conflicted with those values. When I participated from a perspective of curiosity and I asked more questions and we discussed the situation, it allowed them to own their behavior and learn from it. It created space for them to focus on their behavior instead of Dad's.

This parenting example built on the importance of having a respectful relationship with my sons and together to get clear on the values that are important to us, which inform behavioral expectations. Moreover it is in partnership, not out of *Do it because I said to* but from a place of *This is a value that is important to live by for these reasons.*

Deliverable:

When employees are engaged, they and the team perform at a higher level, with improved business results. When Leaders focus on shared values and act in alignment with those values, they promote engagement.

Chapter 2 Summary:

- Measuring employee engagement is a tried-and-true approach for driving improvements in workplace culture that impact the bottom line.

- Noticing the good creates a positive environment and, through contrast, elevates the importance of critical feedback.

- The consideration of values-based relationships versus transactional relationships is important in creating engagement within teams.

- Another exercise for driving engagement is to ask the team you lead to identify their main barriers to success, then start addressing them.

- Principles for how to grow commitment and a sense of belonging also hold when striving to be a good parent or partner.

Practice:

Review the eight engagement statements. Did you identify a gap in your personal engagement? If so, consider why. What would need to happen for you to score those questions higher? Now consider how you can influence your Leader to help improve your experience in the area where your engagement might be lacking.

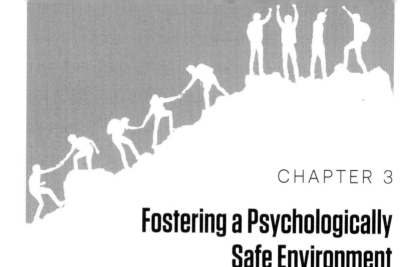

Fostering a Psychologically Safe Environment

uthor Amy Edmondson's *The Fearless Organization*, and Google's "Project Aristotle" (so named in a nod to the Aristotle quote "the whole is greater than the sum of its parts") have elevated our appreciation of psychological safety. In this chapter, I dive into how Leaders can create PS in their teams.

Growing PS starts with measuring it; pertinent to that is a series of assertions of dissatisfaction from *The Fearless Organization* (below):

1. If you make a mistake on this team, it is often held against you.
2. Members of this team are able to bring up problems and tough issues.
3. People on this team sometimes reject others for being different.
4. It is safe to take a risk on this team.
5. It is difficult to ask other members of this team for help.

6. No one on this team would deliberately act in a way that undermines my efforts.

7. Working with members of this team, my unique skills and talents are valued and utilized.

To illustrate PS, let's say you're at a team meeting where the discussion centers on the need to complete a project that's starting to languish. Your Leader is asking how to get back on track. Suppose your personal view is that recent behaviors by your Leader created the issue. Your Leader has been demanding detailed updates from the project team every two weeks, costing you expenditure of time and effort. To answer the questions, each team member has to gather data, update information, create slides and charts, and review all of this with the team. Since your company's systems are antiquated, each update takes a significant amount of digging and research. These requests have disrupted key activities in the project plan, and you believe the project would be close to on track without these frequent updates. Moreover, you feel if your Leader just joined weekly team meetings, observed the work, and sought to support the team, these updates would be unnecessary. You generally like your Leader, but there is much stress around this issue, and you know your Leader is being pressured to deliver on this project as well.

Hearing the request of your Leader for feedback, you ponder what to do. Which course to take. None of your team is speaking up; the room is pinprick quiet. Do you break the silence? This question and what you decide to do is at the heart of the concept of psychological safety.

If you're like me, I have shut down and remained silent many times. My rationalization has gone something like this:

- What's the point? It's not going to get fixed anyway.

- If I speak up, I run the risk of alienating my boss, who decides my pay.
- If I speak up, will anybody else support my view? I'm only sure that it's safer to just be quiet.

Instead of contributing a perspective that might be uncomfortable, I bite my tongue. When this happens, my insight is lost, the opportunity to improve remains hidden, and my Leader will largely remain ignorant of my insights. Everyone loses, and the problem persists.

Unfortunately, this scenario is all too common in business. The lack of PS becomes a silent killer, and you start hearing things like "I'll take *no response* as a sign of support." Silence often gets interpreted as agreement when it may actually be just the opposite. When PS isn't present, the failure to speak out greatly limits the collective wisdom of the team, reducing creativity, transparency, innovation, honesty, vulnerability, and trust.

Below are my top eight recommendations of potential solutions that Leaders can adopt to grow PS:

1. Establish expectations for team members to constructively challenge me and each other.
2. Avoid saying no.
3. Be the last to share your opinion; instead, manage the energy of the room.
4. Acknowledge and encourage constructive challenge.
5. Don't judge.
6. Acknowledge positive behavior.
7. Admit when you're wrong.
8. Promote a learning culture.

Establish Expectations for Constructive Challenge

Early in their tenure, Leaders need to clearly establish that they expect their team members to think critically, creatively, and independently. Most importantly, they expect them to share their thoughts and respectfully challenge both the Leader and their teammates. Setting this expectation and detailing the benefits not only encourages this behavior, but it also establishes constructive challenge as a team value.

One way a Leader can set these expectations is to gather the team and lead them in a discussion comparing two scenarios:

1. When someone on the team expresses agreement with an approach, what does that tell us? What have we learned?
2. When someone on the team challenges the approach, what is the value?

We then start making the lists. Below is my summary of the contrast in the value of each scenario.

Agreement on the Approach	Challenging the Approach
Either the approach is supported, or employees are unwilling to challenge	The challenger is thinking critically
Hopefully, the approach seems reasonable	The challenger is engaged in the subject
	The entire team is able to consider the merits of the challenge
	Discussion is created, and others may feel more courage to share their ideas
	The team considers the approach more deeply

Agreement on the Approach	Challenging the Approach
	Because of the additional discussion, there's greater commitment to the final solution
	Trust is created as the team mulls over the idea together
	Inclusion is promoted as fear is reduced
	Generally, the final solution is superior

Considering these contrasting lists, the team readily sees the difference, and the Leader can make a logical argument in support of critical thinking where all team members share their perspectives freely. For the team, speaking up and challenging becomes a value—and an expectation.

Avoid Saying No

It's rare that a situation calls for a Leader to provide a quick, definite "no." Exceptions: when urgency requires speed and decisiveness, or when a path forward is not up for debate. These situations are rare; 99 percent of the time, a quick no isn't necessary. So, why would we want to avoid a no? A no sends the message that we need Leaders to make decisions, and all should be routed through them. It puts the responsibility solely in the Leader's hands and removes others' responsibility. It also says that others don't have to think through consequences of

> A "no" puts the responsibility solely in the Leader's hands and removes others' responsibility.

options, don't have to think critically about what's best—the Leader will do it. Saying a flat *no* further establishes an authority structure that subordinates followers. And it prohibits a thorough consideration of the question.

When a Leader instead engages in discussion, it invites input, demonstrates respect, and displays the Leader's receptivity to critical thought and others' viewpoints. But the positive effect on the team is even more acute. It honors their perspectives, invites them to participate, and creates ownership. It says, "Let's consider this together, united by trying to do the right thing." No longer can anyone hide behind the authority of the Leader who makes the decisions. They are now expected to think for themselves and share ownership of the decisions.

So how should the Leader approach employee input? Curiosity and open-ended questions are the key, using such language as "Tell me the details of what you want to do." "What are the benefits of doing that?" "What are potential negative ramifications?" "What other approaches have you considered, if any?" "Who might it also be good to run this suggestion by?" "What are the short- and long-term risks, and how would you propose to mitigate them?" "What are the benefits in the short and long term?"

Most of the time, the Leader won't even have to weigh in with an opinion but rather just help others process the issues by asking questions. With this approach, the follower can walk away, assured the plan is valid and supported, knowing that there's more work to do to answer relevant questions, or realizing that limitations compel the need for a different direction.

The important thing is that the Leader didn't make the decision but helped facilitate a thorough analysis. This generally also creates a positive sense of self-esteem in the follower. The replacement of a definite "no" with a process of curiosity and exploration by the Leader is a powerful tool in promoting psychological safety.

Be the last to share your opinion and instead, manage the Energy of the Room

This guidance is, in general, for when a team is in a meeting where discussions are taking place. In such a setting, Leaders need to be aware that their positions will naturally bias the team or some members of it. If a Leader wants everyone to think critically and the unique perspectives of team members to be shared, the wise course is to remain quiet and fully allow the opinions of others to be expressed first.

This behavior sends the additional message that this is a team and that all perspectives are welcome and valid. It creates space for all members to consider the situation as equals, putting aside the natural tendency to give greater weight to the opinions of the person in authority. Leaders speaking last is a natural method to delegate authority. It helps create a safe environment and cultivate psychological safety.

Instead of speaking in the meeting, the Leader should pay attention to the energy in the room. Are people sharing openly, and is conversation acknowledging perspectives and building on them? Are anyone's ideas being minimized, or are individuals being shamed? Has everyone been given a chance to share? Is the conversation engaging and is there a "can do" spirit, or is the team getting caught up in negativity? The Leader should be tuned into the team's energy and act in the role of facilitator to help ensure a positive, collaborative atmosphere.

When Judy is shut down, a good Leader can intervene with "Let's go back to what Judy was saying for a minute. Judy, can you please complete your thoughts?" If comments turn the energy to the negative, the Leader can say, "Yes, we have some challenges, but let's focus on what we can control and remember what our objective is."

In the end, I recommend the seventeenth verse of the *Tao Te Ching*: It states, "The great leader speaks little. He never speaks carelessly. He works without self-interest and leaves no trace. When all is finished, the people say, 'We did it ourselves.'"

Acknowledge and Encourage Constructive Challenge

One of the best gifts Leaders can receive, especially early in their tenure, is for someone to disagree with them publicly. This provides the Leader an opportunity to promote this behavior. They can say something like, "I want to take a moment to thank Bill for sharing. He offered a perspective that we haven't heard yet and that isn't easy to do. On this team we value independent thought and constructive challenge, and Bill just demonstrated that. So, thank you, Bill, and now let's talk about what he just shared."

Acknowledging the challenge in this way affirms that it's not only safe to challenge, but also encouraged. It reinforces this value. Moreover, by identifying something that may feel uncomfortable, it makes the team more self-aware, which liberates them to move past their discomfort.

Do Not Judge

For much of my adult life, I've realized the destructive nature of "good" or "bad" labels—characterizing people in such a way that it instills a perception of good or bad. Judging another person colors the conversation and creates bias. When you judge someone, you pigeonhole that individual in a category. And this category has a way of following people around.

For example, if you refer to Jerry as "contentious," you immediately create an image of him as a person who just likes to argue, who's combative and unproductive. A nonjudgmental alternative would be to strictly stay with the observable facts: "In a recent team meeting, there were three ideas shared. Jerry disagreed with all three but offered no suggestion of his own." In this description, you communicated facts without judgment, only a statement of the observable behavior for consideration. Additionally, judgment is often a barrier to improvement. When you judge, it creates a strong emotion of shame, which then clouds your ability to examine a behavior clearly.

Some months back, I listened to an interview with Liane Davey, author of *The Good Fight: Use Productive Conflict to Get Your Team and Organization Back on Track*. Liane spoke about the evils of judging.

She established a rule that had eluded me and that I found insightful. She said when describing behaviors, to stick to nouns and verbs; when you start using adjectives, you're judging. Simple yet profound and practical, her rule has given me a principle to apply and to teach others.

The bottom line is that everyone wants a fair shot. All of us want to be creators of our own reputation, not victimized by the characterizations of others. Therefore, I teach sensitivity to this issue. When a team member refers to someone as "contentious," other team members should stop and ask, for examples: "What did Alexandra do that caused you to describe her this way?" Maybe she argued every point made in the last meeting. Maybe she raises concerns but doesn't offer any solutions. Maybe she sat there with crossed arms and made comments under her breath. Whatever the case, these are the specific, observable facts to share in place of judgmental adjectives. Then others can decide for themselves.

> . . . when describing behaviors, stick to nouns and verbs; when you start using adjectives, you're judging.

As this may be a hard habit to break, it becomes important for team members to remind each other to replace adjectives with nouns and verbs, sticking to observable behaviors. That not only cuts down on creating false reputations, but it also promotes a psychologically safe environment, as people know the team values not judging each other.

The topic of nonjudgment isn't complete unless we also acknowledge the negative impact of *self*-judging. When we beat ourselves up for having taken an action that we realize was flawed—for being stupid—we're now shaming ourselves. Consequently, emotions like fear will color our future behaviors. We now guard against looking stupid, and we stuff our perspectives to avoid looking bad. Moreover, beating ourselves up isn't pleasant, and doing so will stifle our ability to learn from our behaviors. When, instead, I consider how I acted and what I will do next time, I'm more likely to learn and grow. I encourage everyone to be aware of and guard against self-judgment.

Acknowledge Positive Behavior

People tend to be expert at focusing on the negative. Often, some of the best performers are perfectionists, who lock in on spotting what's wrong. While it's important to expose errors, our human tendency is to focus on the negative and miss all the good that is also present. This can be draining. When you as a Leader only notice the bad, feedback starts falling on deaf ears. When a Leader at least as often notices the good, this adds credibility when they then have to share negative feedback.

One of the most effective ways to create engagement, fearlessness, and psychological safety is for a Leader to appreciate positive behaviors. For positive feedback to be effective, it needs to be thoughtful, substantial, and sincere. If it's forced and unsubstantial or insecure, its value is lost.

Dozens of positive things happen every day that go unnoticed and unacknowledged. This leaves people wondering how they're doing and concluding that "no news is good news." So, they become motivated to just not screw up instead of

being motivated to contribute. By consciously acknowledging the positive, a Leader sets an example for the entire team to emulate. This influence is multiplicative. This is critical because there's no more meaningful compliment than one you receive from someone you work beside every day who has firsthand knowledge of your contributions.

The great thing about noticing the positive is that it's enjoyable. A Leader who does this is attuned to gratitude, and living gratefully is a powerful elixir. It creates a feeling that employees are cared about, people know that their extra efforts will be acknowledged, and is a catalyst for psychological safety.

Admit When You're Wrong:

Let's first dispel any presumption that Leaders cannot make mistakes or show vulnerability or that admitting a mistake is a sign of weakness. This is the opposite of good Leadership. For more detailed supporting information, read the collective works of University of Houston professor Brene Brown, the author of six #1 best sellers. The truth is, when a Leader makes a mistake and admits it, it results in many positives, including:

- It humanizes them: "They are like us."
- It demonstrates personal responsibility.
- It makes it okay to err and, by extension, not okay to hide an error.
- It shows integrity and creates a transparency that enables real progress.

The fact of the matter is that most often, others will know when a Leader has erred; by not admitting it, Leaders will only be fooling themselves and undercutting their integrity.

Promote a Learning Culture

You may be familiar with the recently popular phrase "fail fast." The intent of it is to destigmatize failure in order to try new things and learn from them. Failure teaches us. It's also a way to shine a spotlight fast on the most challenging issues so as not to defer them to the end and incur the much more costly experience of failing late.

If an organization emphasizes the need to learn both as a business and as individuals, it enables so many other positive behaviors. People are expected to try things out. Fear of failure is reduced. Giving and receiving feedback becomes a welcomed practice. Also, a learning culture destigmatizes failure as long as there is learning, and this grows PS.

When something doesn't work out, the question should always be, "What did you/we learn?" And "How will we leverage this knowledge for the future?" In this way, we highlight the long-term value of learning. This, in turn, then minimizes shame associated with the act of failing. When learning is a strong priority, people more readily welcome feedback because that too supports learning.

Finally, these eight tips for creating psychological safety for your team apply equally as well in life. These suggestions will help create a thoughtful, respectful partnership with your significant other, your friends, your family, and in your community. Have you ever thought: *I just wish my partner would admit that they screwed up*. Or, *I just wish we could have a respectful conversation*. When you follow this advice and expect others to be more forthright with you, what results is the blossoming of safety, candor and authenticity in your relationships.

Deliverable:

This chapter reiterates the value of an environment that is psychologically safe. I shared eight tips on creating a psychologically safe culture. Each practical tip can be executed by a Leader with their team, even if the tips aren't practiced by the broader organization.

Chapter 3 Summary:

This chapter outlined eight suggestions for creating psychological safety. They hinge on a Leader's ability to recognize the value of PS and take steps to promote it and reduce fear. But an environment of psychological safety is a plus in any environment whatsoever. Create it in your family, at your church, or in walking down the street and talking to neighbors. Feeling safe with others reduces anxiety, eliminates distractions, and enables connection at a level that breeds fulfillment in life.

Practice:

Review these steps, assessing how they apply in any part of your life, starting with your team. Do employees actively participate? And when challenging each other and authority, do they appear at ease? Do employees robustly participate in meetings? Try applying one or two out of the eight suggestions to create additional PS. If you feel your environment lacks PS, then take the definition of PS and share it with your team; state your intention to improve. Present these nine steps to the team, commit to improving, and ask for their help.

As mentioned above, try out a few of these steps—ones you feel most drawn to or that will help the most—in other situations in your life.

Creating Followership

The saying "People don't leave their company; they leave their boss" is true in my experience. In 2002, I left my company because my boss had become completely numb to my concerns, unwilling to take action to address obvious organizational dysfunction. In agreement with me on the broad decisions that were affecting my ability to effectively lead, he was nevertheless not willing to challenge his leaders. One such decision he left unchallenged was to lay off two maintenance employees to cut costs. Once they were gone, maintenance resources were no longer available to fix leaks in die-casting machines, so oil leaked. Oil covered the floor, creating safety issues, and necessitated extra cleanup time by operators. The year these employees were let go, we spent their salaries paying for additional hydraulic fluid wasted due to equipment neglect. I supplied the data identifying this problem, but the decision to understaff maintenance stood.

Originally my boss had been great to work for. He both challenged me and trusted in my judgment. Inspired by a desire to make a difference and earn his trust, I worked long hours to lead my team. Motivated, we created an operation that was continuously driving improvement and seeking new ways to more efficiently meet customers' expectations. Over time however, new executive leadership came in with the focus on short-term costs. With ground rules changing and in order to meet their expectations, my boss became focused on costs; people became a target for cost reduction. Realizing that this was not an environment for me, I started looking for a company with an engaging culture, where people mattered.

My search started with *Fortune* magazine's annual rating of Top 100 Companies to Work For. This led me to employment in a company whose values were documented, taught, and guided decision-making. This, in turn, established an empowering culture and attracted employees who shared these values. My Leader was committed to creating strong relationships with her team and responsive to their ideas and insights. We shared a hunger to drive improvement, and the team challenged each other on how best to move forward. With enthusiasm I began working long hours, eager to make a difference. I had purpose, engagement, and passion, and together we made huge progress. My Leader's judgment, willingness to be challenged, and support of me and the team created a strong sense of followership, enabling achievement of potential.

How should we assess the effectiveness of a Leader? Instead of debating various sides of this subject, let's recognize a few authorities on the question. As Buckingham and Goodall say, "A leader is someone who has followers, pure and simple." They base this assertion on studies that show people are bad assessors of others but good assessors of their own experience. Therefore, an assessment of a Leader becomes valid only by understanding others' (followers') experience of the Leader.

In *Multipliers: How the Best Leaders make Everyone Smarter*, Liz Wiseman sees developing relationships, being curious, and challenging others to achieve what they didn't think was possible as the framework for Leaders to get the most out of others. Thus, Wiseman seems to agree that the effectiveness of Leaders is defined by their ability to influence others (have followers).

Bill George in *Authentic Leadership* agrees that Leadership isn't a list of attributes or styles that will make you a Leader if you adopt them. He defines great Leaders by their authenticity: "Authentic leaders genuinely desire to serve others through their leadership. They are more interested in empowering the people they lead to make a difference than they are in power.... They lead with purpose, meaning, and values. They build enduring relationships with people. Others follow them because they know where they stand."

Finally, Bruce D. Schneider, the founder of the Institute for Professional Excellence in Coaching (iPEC), created a model for assessing attitude called the Energy Leadership Index (ELI). This model correlates predominant levels of attitude with one's ability to influence and lead. He called this "Energy Leadership." Thus, completely independently, Schneider also agrees that Leadership relates to one's ability to influence others.

Additional basis for this view of leadership is supported by expectations of millennials to have meaning at work, the importance of understanding the "Why," as detailed by Simon Sinek, and the increasing complexity of global organizations for distributed decision-making; to be nimble and competitive, organizations need to distribute authority. This requires Leaders to be influencers and humbly share their authority. In short, strong followership is the measure of great Leaders.

If you agree with these great minds, then it's important to determine a method for assessing followership.

Some years ago, I worked with an HR professional, who was a student of human behavior. We worked together on the project to determine how to assess strength of followership. My colleague reviewed pertinent research and proposed relevant questions, which we tested and revised. We then created a process for administering the survey, which you will read about in the following pages.

It will become evident that more than just providing information on a Leader's current strength of followership, the process I detail, merely by being followed, will grow followership. This underscores a recurring theme in this book that intentions matter: the process works because it demonstrates a desire to receive feedback, a willingness to use the feedback for growth, and *a vulnerability* in asking followers for their continuing support.

Having "Leader" or "Manager" in your title doesn't make you a Leader. Merriam-Webster defines Leader as "a person who has commanding authority or influence." *Companies who follow this definition and expect Leaders to have "commanding authority" in my opinion will ultimately fail.* I believe this definition is outdated—it's not twenty-first-century—and "commanding authority" chokes out rich discussion, limits engagement, and drives away skilled, intelligent, independent employees. They turn to employers that tap into their skills. Leaders do not have infinite capacity and when authority is not shared, the company will be limited by the Leader. By distributing authority and then focusing on organizing instead of directing the teams, a collaborative Servant Leader expands this capacity. In this chapter I embrace this updated definition of a Leader as influencer and a person with strong followership.

> Leaders do not have infinite capacity and when authority is not shared, the company will be limited by the Leader.

The following details our method for assessing strength of followership.

Followership Assessment Process (FAP):

1. Requesting a follower assessment: A Leader identifies a facilitator to manage the FAP. My foundational belief is that assessing followership is most productive when treated as a development process rather than a measure of merit. The result is a growth mindset instead of a merit review; the latter breeds judgment and defensiveness. Moreover, it is with the intent of personally growing that a Leader requests this assessment. So, to have an individual Leader request this process versus the manager assigning the assessment is foundationally important to success.

2. Identifying objectives and participants: The Leader and facilitator meet to discuss desired objectives and identify a team of individuals who will complete

the followership questionnaire. Those identified should be led primarily by the Leader but should also include some peers as well as the Leader's Leader—thus providing a richer spectrum of input and an opportunity to identify where the Leader treats people differently based on their role in the organization.

3. Requesting participation: The Leader then individually approaches all those identified to ask if they would be willing to commit to the survey. In this conversation, the Leader shares the overall process, the role of the facilitator, and necessary details about the pending anonymous survey. The Leader also stresses a personal desire to grow, emphasizing the importance of the input to help identify potential growth areas. This conversation creates a receptivity to feedback as well as producing a higher response rate (we've experienced 90 percent) of participation. These five-to-ten-minute conversations take place with each person participating in the survey.

4. Sending out the survey: The standard questionnaire goes out, with a timeframe for completing it. It captures responses on a 5-point scale with 1 = "rarely true," 3 = "sometimes true," and 5 = "consistently true." The survey questions that we recommend (based on Cate's research) are as follows:

    1) I believe this Leader's intentions are good.

    2) I have confidence in this Leader's professional judgment.

    3) I trust that this Leader has the courage to do the right thing even when it's difficult, unpopular, or against their personal interests.

4) I believe this Leader cares about my wellbeing.

5) I can depend on this Leader to do their part.

6) Interactions with this Leader give me greater confidence in my own ability to succeed.

7) This Leader helps motivate my efforts to contribute effectively.

8) This Leader is a constructive influence and helps bring out the best in me.

5. Organizing the results: Based on reviewing the data, clarifying with individuals any responses that may be unclear to gain deeper understanding, and scrubbing the comments to ensure anonymity, the facilitator creates a summary report.

6. Reviewing results and creating growth objectives: The facilitator then delivers the summary report to the Leader, and together they identify where opportunities for growth lie. In so doing, they determine the *what* and the *when*, and how to follow up. This becomes the Leader's development plan.

7. Following up with respondents: The Leader then closes the loop with the respondents by thanking each individually for providing feedback; the Leader also shares specific intentions for growth and expresses a willingness to receive feedback in the future if the respondent sees any fallback or slide into unwanted historic behavior.

8. Plan for following up: Finally, the facilitator and the Leader plan for future follow-up on their progress, with the option to repeat the survey sometime down the road.

Followership is really about people having respect for you and is partly determined by the respect you show for them and your willingness to serve them by addressing barriers to their success. The methodology described above is simply a process for saying, *I care about how you experience me and want to know how I can improve to strengthen our relationship.* Demonstrating you respect and care creates a reciprocating karma of mutual consideration. And it strengthens the ability to influence.

You don't need to follow this process to create this same connection outside of work. The steps above simply establish vulnerability and receptivity while asking how you can lead more effectively. The same can be created in everyday life through candidly acknowledging that you don't have the answers while advancing a curiosity in what others have to teach you.

Deliverable:

This chapter establishes the importance of followership for a high-performing Leader. I introduce a process for measuring followership that helps grow followership in the administration of it.

Chapter 4 Summary:

The steps for assessing strength of followership are listed below:

1. Request assessment.
2. Identify objectives and participants.
3. Request participation.
4. Send out the survey.
5. Organize the results.
6. Review results and create growth objectives.
7. Follow up with respondents.
8. Make a plan for follow-up.

Practice:

I invite you to engage in this process by finding a facilitator to support you. **Scan** the QR code below to take you to documents that define this process and give you forms your team can use for the survey.

B y 2009, I'd developed an approach to Leadership that felt right for me. Having twenty years of Leadership experience under my belt, I took a Plant Leader role at a small manufacturing site with about 125 employees, half of whom were in manufacturing. I was the Leader of an experienced team who were particularly proficient at being hands-on. They placed a high priority on developing relationships with their team members and promoting personal responsibility. In a word, they were Servant Leaders, in the job to "make a difference."

Together, we focused on not shying away from difficult discussions. On the contrary, we met them head on—handling them conversationally, promoting direct, respectful communication and teaching these skills to our employees. We actively worked to create an environment that empowered employees in solving their issues themselves. When an employee brought us a difficult interpersonal challenge, we would start with, "What have you done about this so far?" "Have you had a conversation with the other person?" We recognized that if, as Leaders, we intervened, we might damage the relationship between the two antagonists. To avoid this, we taught, encouraged, and role-played how to have difficult but productive conversations. We felt like this was a skill that each team member should possess in a healthy workplace.

This culture of direct, respectful communication grew within our manufacturing environment. Employees took responsibility for overcoming personal discomfort to communicate—vulnerably and authentically. Over time, operators overcame fear to give feedback to peers, engineers, their Leaders, and even me, their Plant Leader.

One day I had a front-line Leader come into my office, asking if I had a moment to talk. As she shut the door behind her, I held my breath, knowing that what she was about to say had been wearing on her. She recalled a recent meeting where something I said had unwittingly touched a nerve. Overcoming discomfort, she shared how she had interpreted my words, how they made her feel.

As I listened to her frustration accompanied by anxiety at giving me feedback, I felt a deep appreciation for her forthrightness and that she was a Leader of others. I listened, asked a few clarifying questions, and empathized with her interpretation. My statement, I acknowledged, was sloppy and confusing. Thankfully, I said, she came straight to me and gave me the opportunity to reflect. I then explained the intended meaning while conceding her interpretation. We had a great exchange, and in the end, I thanked her for holding me accountable, encouraging her to do so in the future.

Some weeks later, I asked her permission to tell this story. Receiving her nod of approval, I shared it with every new employee on our team—pointing to it as an example of the culture we embraced—and emphasizing the expectation that if they felt in conflict with a teammate, they would similarly practice direct communication.

Let's consider the opposite scenario; what might have happened if this employee hadn't come to me but instead shared her frustration with her peers? Amid the rumbles of discontent, coworkers, hearing secondhand accounts of her experience, might have drawn unwarranted conclusions about my character. It could have silently created a reputation for me, undermining my credibility and ability to effectively lead. I would have been hard pressed to know what I'd done!

This example underscores the importance of a culture of candor. Directness creates trust. Complaining to someone else creates a culture of gossip that undermines trust and is like a cancer, disabling a healthy culture. Moreover, directness is regenerative in that those prone to victimization and slander find it uncomfortable. It forces them to either learn how to be respectfully direct or they leave the team. Consequently, Servant Leaders who take feedback well and grow the skills of giving and receiving feedback in others are uniquely capable of fostering a healthy atmosphere.

In my experience, as reflected in employee surveys, which are one way to measure the health of a culture, direct-labor manufacturing employees (those who work directly on the product) as a group consistently score among the lowest. I believe this is explained by the restrictive nature of their job, in that they have to be on the line at certain times and are directly accountable for each minute at work. Yet, thanks to the Leader who gave me direct feedback and other Leaders like her, our manufacturing team scored 97 percent satisfaction in our survey results. This was roughly 15 percent higher than the company average. Clearly, this focus of direct, respectful, authentic communication created a great environment for employees.

While the culture-survey results were gratifying, the best by-product was that—without having to include Leaders—the team exercised their personal initiative to resolve problems that cropped up. They felt a responsibility for a great culture and overcame personal discomfort to protect it. *As a not-insignificant aside, this culture also produced superior business results.* Our plant had an identical manufacturing line to that in another plant. While we did not encourage comparisons, the fact of the matter is that our yields were several percent higher, as was our efficiency in output per hour. Good cultures create high performance.

> **A culture of authenticity and directness motivates the team to take responsibility for their relationships and frees Leaders to focus on improvement not conflict resolution.**

Think of how many times, as a Leader, you get pulled into issues connected to interpersonal conflict or misunderstanding. Now think of what your life would be like if you could reduce them by 90 percent. Being a Leader in this environment was the most fulfilling experience of my career. With issues handled organically, it freed up the entire Leadership team. If, prior to this, we spent less than 10 percent of our time on improvement projects, now we spent 25 percent or more. Consequently, fire-fighting went down, yields and productivity rose, and our business success was unparalleled. In manufacturing the same product, we quickly outproduced a sister plant, all because we dealt effectively with interpersonal conflict and taught employees to exercise personal responsibility.

If this is the kind of team you want, the kind of Leader you want to be, or even the type of parent you aspire to, *Discovering Leaders Within* is the book for you. No one says it's easy, but it's within your reach. Contrary to popular belief, great Leaders don't have to be the smartest, the most articulate, or the best strategists. They don't need an impressive list of competencies; don't need to be the most inspirational. But what they do need is to be approachable, self-aware, and committed to goals that transcend personal needs while not avoiding discomfort. There are many paths to achieving this, but being a Servant Leader with a basis in strong E.I. is a great founding principle. And since E.I. can be taught, it enables Leadership Development (LD) programs with the right focus to grow great Leaders.

Part 1 of this book establishes a common thirst for this type of Leader, shows the importance of humility, and then details the seven-step HUMan-Based-LEadership approach to LD with a key foundation in building individual and team E.I.

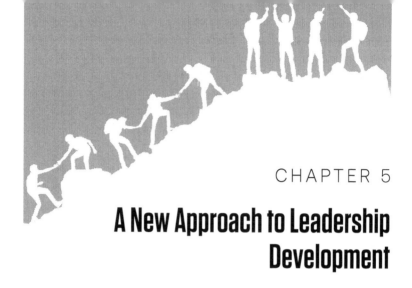

CHAPTER 5

A New Approach to Leadership Development

Valuing follower priorities and business priorities over personal interests characterizes the concept of a "Servant Leader." The *MIT Sloan Management Review* recently studied the factors that have the greatest impact on creating a positive company culture:

- Employees feel respected
- Leaders are supportive
- Leaders live core values

These three attributes happen to coincide identically with the focuses of Servant Leaders.

Many other studies I listed in the bibliography demonstrate a correlation between Servant Leadership and better employee performance, increased team confidence, better utilization of employee strengths, egalitarianism, increased followership, and improved overall organizational performance. Moreover, it fosters long-term exceptional performance and a built-in succession-planning mechanism.

So, the question becomes, how do you develop Servant Leaders? Ultimately, healthy adults, no matter our age, have brains that are neuroplastic: we can change the way we think and behave. Therefore, all of us are teachable. But learning to be a Servant Leader isn't taught by simply following traditional LD curriculum, acquiring knowledge, or implementing tools and techniques. It starts with self-awareness: looking inside yourself to understand your values, motivations, fears, assumptions, judgments, and the like. In addition to self-awareness, self-management, other awareness and relationship management are the primary component of emotional intelligence. Growing E.I. is foundational to becoming a great Servant Leader and high E.I. is the factor that most highly correlates with high-performing Leaders and superior business results (*Emotional Intelligence 2.0* by Bradberry and Greaves). LD programs that don't include developing E.I. are simply incomplete.

> (Servant Leadership) starts with self-awareness: looking inside oneself to understand one's values, motivations, fears, preconceptions, judgments, and the like.

As I embarked on my role as a Leadership Development Program Manager, I was struck—as contrasted with basic research in the field—by the failings of the "traditional approaches" I'd personally experienced. For example, while traditional programs target achieving growth in specific competencies, *research indicated the contrary:* that to focus on addressing weakness does *not* improve business outcomes. It's more effective in elevating business performance to leverage strengths (*Nine Lies about Work*, Buckingham and Goodall). **Appendix 1** details what I believe are the inherent challenges in traditional approaches, contrasted with the HUM-B-LE approach.

How do we know that traditional LD programs aren't generally effective? In the *Development Dimensions International (DDI) 2018 Global Leadership Forecast*, nearly 26,000 Leaders and 2,550 Human Resource (HR) Professionals from 2,488 organizations responded to a range of questions on leadership. From CEOs, asked what issues would command their attention in the coming year, the top-scored response was "Developing 'Next Gen' leaders." That same report concluded that in terms of Leadership quality, improvement looks dim: there has been "little progress six years running."

Three years later, DDI updated the survey in the "CEO Leadership Report 2021." That report similarly highlighted top executives' concern for "the quality of frontline and mid-level leadership." And it stated, "Bench strength is at an all-time low as companies struggle to fill critical positions." *Why was so little progress made in three years when this was a top objective?*

The *Harvard Business Review* in April of 2019 published an article, "The Future of Leadership Development." It stated that while "companies spend heavily on executive education," they "often get a meager return . . . because business schools . . . aren't adept at teaching the soft skills vital for success today . . . Most education programs focus on discipline-based skill sets such as strategy development and financial analysis." Outlining a "Skills Transfer Gap," the article concluded that "what's learned is rarely applied."

The picture it paints is that traditional LD training programs aren't effective, even while the business need has been great.

Discovering Leaders Within answers the need for a better, more effective approach to LD. In three years of practicing it, we have found it creates more effective Leaders, as demonstrated by a significant improvement in employee engagement and psychological safety. The value of these metrics and their connection to improved business results is detailed in Gallup's work on employee engagement, and Amy Edmondson's research, and Google's "Project Aristotle" (see Chapter 3), which investigate psychological safety.

Deliverable:

This chapter was meant to question the effectiveness of traditional LD programs and to suggest a revised approach that is documented in Part 2 of this book. While I've shared broad data on dissatisfaction with LD, each company is different and the point is to be conscious of this topic and challenge your approach if it is not serving your organization.

Chapter 5 Summary

Surveys of business leaders reveal that while developing future leaders is a high priority, we don't seem to be creating them. Nor are we making improvements in this arena. This suggests that traditional approaches to Leadership development are ineffective and a new, fruitful approach is needed.

Practice

Consider the Leadership Development programs in your organization. How tailored are they to the specific needs of the students? How long have they been in place and, how effective are they in growing better Leaders in the long-term? How is their effectiveness measured? If the answers to any of these questions are unfulfilling, consider challenging and revising your approach to LD.

CHAPTER 6

The Case for Emotional Intelligence

Have you ever had a marvelous boss who was trusting, supportive, and empowering as long as things went smoothly, but with increased stress would grasp for more control, requiring that you now run previously delegated decisions by him?

I have experienced this so regularly in thirty years that it feels almost like it's in a leadership textbook. Moreover, it has happened in a variety of situations, not just caused by business downturns. One time, this reaction was triggered by an acquisition that tied up cash. Another time the instigation was a new performance metric for profit per employee; my Leaders wanted to hit the goal by temporarily restricting all spending. Simple fears of a potential business downturn, even when the sales team isn't projecting long-term change in demand, has also touched off this reaction.

Each time, it felt disempowering. I and my team always wound up with added-on work, having to justify and document proposals we typically just acted on. And it generally felt like a fearful, defensive reaction on the part of leaders who desperately wanted to gain personal control over a perceived crisis.

So why is grasping for control by executives such a common response to stress? Could subordinates suddenly not be trusted to use their own judgment? Was there not a moment or a day in which to bring Leaders in to share the challenge, including them in the discussion of a path forward? Wouldn't this unleash greater creativity, leverage cumulative knowledge, and intensify commitment?

It's also important to recognize the negative long-term consequences of this power-grabbing behavior. It can ultimately lead to turnover of the highest performers, who no longer feel they are getting respect and autonomy. Numerous examples demonstrate that companies who react best to crises show consistency of commitment to their values. If empowerment is important before the crisis, crises are best handled with inclusion. A crisis can actually motivate employees to unify in planning a response. And the whole team steps up to the challenge.

One example of this is the highly rated Bob Chapman, # 3 CEO worldwide in an *Inc.* magazine article. Running Barry-Wehmiller, a St. Louis-based global manufacturer of capital goods, he created a culture of family and a commitment to societal, in addition to business, health. When the 2009 recession hit, and it hit hard with an overnight drop of 35 percent in orders, he leveraged his employees instead of ignoring them. In alignment with the company principles he asked, "What would a caring family do?" The answer was, "Everyone would pitch in."

So, everyone shared in furloughs (mandatory temporary leaves of absence, as contrasted with layoffs); employees were allowed to modify the duration of the furloughs among themselves as long as the overall goals were met. This meant that a financially stable employee could give time to a team member whose furlough created hardship. Thus, even in this crisis, relationships were strengthened, not severed; jobs were saved (not one single job was lost); and employee loyalty was multiplied. Moreover, when demand came back, Barry-

Wehmiller was uniquely positioned to capitalize on it with the force of the experienced team that had not been diluted by layoff. In the entire history of the company, 2010 became the best year.

In times of economic downturn, thoughtful Leaders pause to consider the identity of the company. This brings a type of corporate self-awareness, the first attribute of E.I. And they weigh carefully how to best handle their response. This is the self-management aspect of E.I.

Emotional Intelligence (E.I.) is about consciousness. It's about being self-aware that an event has triggered strong emotions and taking time to pause before reacting. E.I. Leaders don't grasp for control, but rather considering other stakeholders, they seek out the perspective of followers, engaging their collective skills, backgrounds, knowledge, and creativity. And they proceed in a way that shares information, creates ownership and understanding, and strengthens relationships. If tough decisions must be made, the team understands why; as partners, they overcome the crisis together with management. Through this approach, the E.I. Leader is able to turn the crisis into a rallying point.

I believe that an LD program with a foundation in growing individual and team E.I. is the antidote to knee-jerk reactions to difficult challenges. E.I. leads to consistent, values-based behaviors that are the bedrock for long-term success. E.I. Leaders treat relationships as critical. They reflect, engage, listen, and challenge teammates to find solutions. And when they misstep, they're receptive to

> The trick is to get past the ego and its defensiveness, and to connect with a vulnerability that enables learning.

feedback, acknowledge their error, and take corrective action. E.I. Leaders are equipped to lead effectively in good times and bad. "We can get through this because we trust each other, and we trust our Leader," is the basis for enduring success.

Deliverable:

Emotional intelligence is the attribute which is most correlated with high performance including Leadership effectiveness. This chapter makes the case that E.I. should be a foundational aspect of any LD program.

Chapter 6 Summary:

Emotional Intelligence enables people to not simply react but to pause and consider a thoughtful response. With this skill, Leaders can grow purpose, build dedication, and ensure commitment in times of crisis. In contrast, cultures and respect are undermined when inept leaders mechanically react to crises.

Practice:

If you need to address behavioral issues with someone, first consider that person's perspective. Where is the other person coming from? With what needs? What is the observable behavioral evidence that you need to reference in the meeting? Prepare by thinking about how to communicate the behavior and then ask for the employee's perspective on the matter. Prepare to provide feedback that creates space for the employee as you problem-solve together.

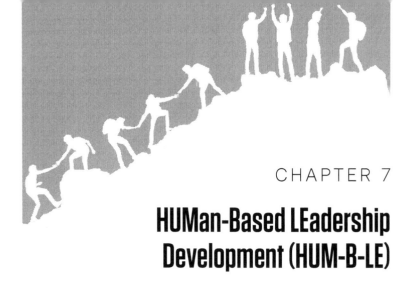

CHAPTER 7

HUMan-Based LEadership Development (HUM-B-LE)

As a profession, physical therapy is designed to help improve the health of the client. Therapists are expert in the function of the human body: the interaction of muscles, tendons, ligaments, bones, blood flow, nerves, and so on. They know how things should work when someone is healthy. So, in acquiring a new patient, do they start right in on giving that patient exercises to strengthen muscles, stretches to loosen tightness, and manipulations to activate blood flow? No, they first complete a thorough analysis of new patients. Where are they feeling pain? Do they have an adequate range of motion? How strong are they in various muscle groups? What's their balance like and their flexibility? How are they moving and where might they be compensating? The first and most time-consuming aspect of the treatment is the initial assessment to determine the source of the physical disfunction. They diagnose patients before treating them, and they verify improvement before releasing them.

To be effective and efficient, Leadership Development programs should also diagnose before they treat and ensure improvement is a result of their effort. While this takes additional time, it focuses efforts on producing a valuable outcome for the LD student/customers. By initially measuring and diagnosing, it's true that LD professionals have to take additional steps in delivering their services and can't run as many students through the program, but it creates a shared accountability for delivering quality.

Speed versus Effectiveness (Quality)

Let's define the value of an LD program as a combination of speed and effectiveness. Speed measures how quickly training can be delivered to a large number of students. Effectiveness is a measure of the impact the program has on changing Leaders' behavior to deliver improved business results. LD programs should aim to maximize the product of speed and effectiveness.

For this example, let's score speed on a scale of one to five, with a one constituting a low number of professionals going through the process and graduating and five indicating a large number. When we assess effectiveness, we must change the scale a bit because it's possible for the program to be completely ineffective, which means it has zero long-term value. So, the effectiveness scale will start at zero, in the case where a program is completely ineffective at changing Leaders' behavior, and a 5 if it's extremely effective in improving Leaders' behavior and driving results.

Now let's look at the extreme example of a fast but ineffective approach, which can be assessed with the following value equation:

$$Value_{(fast\ and\ ineffective)} = 5\ (fast)\ x\ 0\ (ineffective) = 0$$

As you can see, fast and totally ineffective provides no value.

In contrast, a slow but effective program reaps the alternative product:

$$Value_{(slow\ and\ effective)} = 1\ (slow)\ x\ 5\ (effective) = 5$$

The conclusion is that slow and effective always beats fast and ineffective. Even if the program is slow, there will be value if it's effective. The same cannot be said for a program that's fast but ineffective.

This simple equation may explain why CEOs don't believe their LD programs are effective, even though the need to effectively develop Leaders has consistently been a business priority, receiving billions of dollars of investment annually. LD professionals may be focusing too much on speed and not enough on effectiveness.

> The quality of an LD program is paramount for progress. It trumps a competing motivation for speed.

HUM-B-LE Development is a research-based approach to LD that's more effective than traditional approaches. It was developed after a review of hundreds of sources on the topic of what makes a great Leader and the attributes of an effective LD program. Peer-reviewed research was a primary foundation of this work, and several rounds of application went into the molding of the process I coined as HUM-B-LE.

Before embarking on the application of HUM-B-LE, an organization should first consider how to assess the effectiveness of LD programs. Getting clear on the objectives of an LD program is important because it will focus the LD process. What effect would a better Leader have? Is the goal to improve the culture, to create more engaged employees, to improve Leadership bench strength, or to raise team psychological safety? Or is it improved business results over time?

LD is about tapping into the potential of people to Lead in order to achieve a desired outcome. If the main goal is to grow Leaders that improve business results, research suggests that the following factors correlate with improved business performance:

- Engaged employees
- Psychological safety in the team
- Growing emotional intelligence

These are the attributes I target when assessing the effectiveness of the HUM-B-LE development approach because they can be measured and result in improved business results. Focusing directly on business outcome is harder to correlate with the LD program because it is affected by so many other variables outside of the Leader's control.

Below, a table compares **HUM-B-LE against traditional** approaches. For a more detailed explanation for why we believe "traditional" LD programs have shortcomings, we invite you to reference Appendix 1. This table outlines the differences as we move into subsequent chapters that detail the specific components of HUM-B-LE.

Characteristic	Traditional LD Cohort	HUM-B-LE LD
Value related to participants	Value in networking of disparate Leaders	Value in growing relationships within a Leadership team
Curriculum	Standard Curriculum	Some standard training and some customized to team's needs
Implementation	Individual students implement concepts	Team implements content
Delivery of Training	LD experts deliver content	LD experts partner with team Leader in delivery of content
Timing of class	Content delivered without consideration of timing for its use	Custom approach enables aligning concepts with timing of application
Measure of success	Typically, success is assessed by quality of training experience	Success is measured by impact on the culture enabling business results
Sustainment	Limited follow-up post class	Plan defined for sustained application of Leadership concepts by the team

Results:

I have applied the HUM-B-LE methodology to four teams of Leaders each of whom supports manufacturing operations ranging from eighty to two-hundred-and-twenty employees. In each case, I started with surveys to assess psychological safety and employee engagement; then, three-to-six months after we executed the HUM-B-LE approach, I repeated the survey. From the results, even though each team began with a relatively high engagement level where 86 percent of the responses were positive, the improvement in the scores was still significant. After applying HUM-B-LE, positive responses grew to 92 percent and demonstrated that by applying the HUM-B-LE method, even healthy cultures can be improved upon. Nearly half of the negative responses were converted to positive only three months after Leaders completed the HUM-B-LE development program.

Deliverable:

This chapter helps us recognize that the quality of a LD program is paramount for progress. It must trump a competing goal of speed. Quality without speed still adds value. Speed without quality is a waste of time.

Summary of Chapter 7

- Advantages of "traditional LD programs" are that they drive standardized, efficient training and promote networking with peer Leaders. The primary shortcomings are that they prioritize speed over effectiveness and focus on teaching generic skills to the deficit of addressing Leaders' specific needs.

- An organization should understand what it is trying to accomplish with the LD program. This will influence the focus of the program and the measurement of success.

- The HUM-B-LE approach focuses on the needs of particular teams, delivering content to the team rather than to a disparate group of individual Leaders. A team develops together, and this approach prioritizes effectiveness over speed.

Practice:

Consider situations where you prioritized speed over effectiveness. What were the results? Would you approach the project differently, given an opportunity to do it over? Now, reflect on instances where you prioritized effectiveness over speed. What was the value of this? Would you approach this situation differently in the future?

The HUM-B-LE Methodology

As an Operations Leader, I felt like there was not enough time in the day to get everything done. The job largely consisted of working with my team to define and execute the highest-priority tasks. When influences outside of my team, such as new broad initiatives, mandatory training, or unplanned business challenges, impacted us, it was always an undertaking to figure out how to get them done without throwing us and our priorities off track.

I created the HUMan-Based LEadership development program, based on a sensitivity to this challenge of trying to juggle competing priorities. The philosophy that drove the work was, *how to impart the most critical Leadership skills and address any other current issues that the specific team was facing so as to provide the highest value in the least amount of time.* Diagram 1 illustrates the steps of HUM-B-LE, defined to achieve this goal. What follows the diagram is a concise description of each step. Subsequent chapters detail more deeply how to carry out each step. But here, in a capsule, is an overview:

Diagram 1.

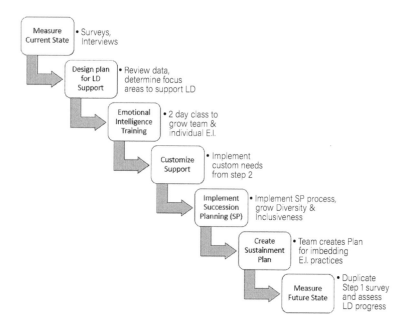

I. **Measure:** This step involves understanding the development needs specific to the client team. To identify growth needs, we measure PS and employee engagement in an initial survey and also interview a subset of Leaders and followers.

2. **Design:** After gathering all the information in the previous step, the LD professional sits down with the core Leader (or Leadership Team), reviews the data, and identifies areas of opportunity. Together they define how to approach key improvement needs. By the end of this step, both the LD professional and team Leader have agreed upon a plan and set improvement goals.

3. **Develop Emotional Intelligence:** This interactive class includes exercises that grow skills in the five components of E.I.: self-awareness, self-management, outside awareness, relationship management, and resilience.

4. **Customize Support:** Based on what was determined in the design step, additional development opportunities are delivered.

5. **Plan for Succession:** This step implements a key succession-planning strategy called the Development Planning Process (DPP), which engages Leader(s) in collectively assessing and supporting growth of future Leaders.

6. **Sustain:** A sustainment plan is developed to assure gains obtained throughout HUM-B-LE development are utilized and not lost after the process is complete.

7. **Measure Future State:** Finally, post completion of the HUM-B-LE development program, the system of metrics utilized in the first step to understand the current state is repeated. This will inform both the Leadership team and the LD professional about the success of the program in improving the impact of Leaders' behaviors toward growing an improved employee experience.

Deliverable:

In a nutshell this chapter outlines the HUM-B-LE development process for growing individual and team Leadership skills. By design, it brings solutions pertinent to the individual team needs without excessive training. And it creates a partnership with the local Leaders in delivery of value-added content.

Chapter 8 Summary:

- There are seven steps of HUM-B-LE development: 1) assess the current state, 2) identify needs and a plan specific to the team, 3) deliver E.I. training, 4) address customized team needs, 5) implement the Development Planning Process, 6) define a plan to sustain improved behaviors, and 7) measure the future progress.

- Two of the steps create a standard approach for growing and improving Leaders: E.I. training and the Development Planning Process. The other steps facilitate understanding and addressing the needs of the team in going through the program, locking in the gains.

- Both the team Leader and the LD professional take ownership of achieving improved Leadership behavior, as indicated by the before/after measurements of the program.

Practice:

Next time you want to teach someone, pause to understand that person's specific circumstances and perspective. Then plan your teaching approach accordingly—to incorporate the specifics of the person's experience—which will maximize the training effectiveness. Make sure your intention to provide value lines up directly with the client's or employee's needs.

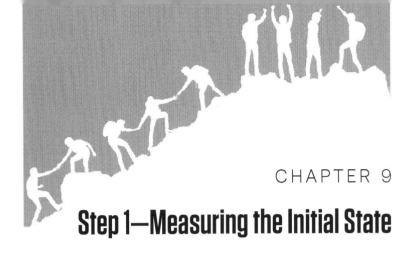

Step 1—Measuring the Initial State

Over my career, I've participated in numerous reorganizations. They begin with leaders dissatisfied with some aspect(s) of business performance. Through whatever analysis, they conclude that the current organization needs redefinition. High-level conversations usually then ensue, birthing a new organizational model. Then comes the difficult task of execution. When the plan is communicated and changes are implemented is where confusion breaks out.

All change—and reorganizations are a significant form of change—creates chaos, at least short-term. Every reorganization has some negative implications; some area that is not served quite as well as in the former state. So, how do we monitor this? How do we hold ourselves accountable for achieving the purpose behind the call for change? In any intentional implementation of change, we need to identify what the purpose is

> **With any business endeavor, it's important to understand if the work is having a positive impact and negative effects are being minimized.**

and how we plan to measure and monitor the results. This allows us to check whether the change has accomplished its purpose and, if not, take additional actions to correct what went wrong or fell short. Not having this evaluation system, we tend to conclude the change was good because it was needed. But did it drive improvement? Without the mechanism to measure the outcome, we really don't know.

With any significant change, it's important to ensure the work is having a positive impact and to identify potentially negative implications. This requires a plan for measuring. More than revealing the true value of the change, monitoring the outcome of the plan creates accountability and helps motivate a more thoughtful planning process.

The endeavor to grow and develop Leaders is no different. LD programs should be clear on the purpose of the program as it relates to improving performance that aligns with meeting business objectives. Moreover, LD professions should partner with local leaders to agree on measures and set goals. This initiates a shared accountability.

So, what's the purpose of your Leadership Development program? Is it to deliver a base level of competency? Is it to get X number of people through the program? Maybe it's to develop Leaders who can create a more fulfilling work environment or to ultimately drive improved business results?

These are important questions that LD program owners and business Leaders need to align on. *The answer to "What do we want to accomplish with the LD program?" will determine what to measure.* The following table lists some potential measures of LD program effectiveness and potential pros and cons.

Measurement	Measurement Type	Pro	Con
Quality of the Training	Survey team of trainees	Easy to get. Measurement is right after training. Useful for improving training content.	Doesn't measure the impact of the training. Not helpful for the team being trained.
Quality of the LD Program	Survey Leadership team	Easy to get. Measurement timing is close to the experience being assessed. Useful for LD team.	Doesn't measure the impact of the program. Not helpful for the team being trained.
Strength of Followership	Assess Followers (See Chapter 4)	Provides a direct measure of the individual Leader's ability to influence. Results provide detail for where to grow. Application of the process helps grow followership.	Time-consuming and requires a facilitator for every leader assessment.
Engagement of the team	Survey broad, extended team	Provides a standard survey backed by research that correlates to business results. Team can create improvement goals.	Needs to be months after LD program (see above). Other factors outside of Leaders' control can impact this.

Measurement	Measurement Type	Pro	Con
Psychological Safety	Survey broad, extended team	Provides a standard survey backed by research that correlates to business results. Team can create improvement goals.	Needs to be months after LD program (see above). Other factors outside of Leaders' control can impact this.
Number of "Ready Now" Leaders	Assess Leadership Team	Measures the results of succession-planning efforts over time. Team can create improvement goals.	Requires a standard process to assess "ready now." This is a long-term measure, taken over one year or more.
Impact on Key Performance Indicators (KPI)	Keep a Standard chart of Team KPIs over time.	Connects LD program directly to business value.	Many other confounding variables and takes time for behavior change to create improved business metrics.

The key to successfully applying measurements to evaluate LD program effectiveness is to define what the organization expects and conduct baseline measures *before* initiating the program. Analyzing measures up front will highlight current opportunities for improvement, create an opening for the Leader and team to set goals, and provide motivation and accountability. Finally, accountability is shared by both the LD team and the Leadership team.

Surveys of how the broader team experienced their local culture yield a standard, proven, quantitative approach. Yet these surveys might not tell the complete picture. To enable a better grasp of the employee experience that can inform the HUM-B-LE approach, you can supplement these surveys with interviews of subsets of employees.

Equipped with survey data and testimonials from employees, the LD team and the Leaders they're supporting have a good picture of the current state and can begin the task of identifying the Leadership skills best suited to address the opportunities. This completes the first Measurement step of the HUM-B-LE process.

Deliverable:

At the end of this step, the team has sufficient data defining the current environment. This enables ownership and goal-setting.

Chapter 9 Summary:

- Measuring the current state is key to a number of things: understanding the opportunity, creating shared goals for improvement, and holding the LD program and the local Leaders responsible for evolving Leader behaviors that improve performance measures.

- Steps for measuring the current state:

  i. LD professionals and local Leaders agree on the survey and send it out to all team members.

2. The LD professional interviews team members to qualitatively understand other opportunities for improvement.

3. The LD professional and local Leaders assess the data, setting long term improvement goals.

Practice:

In your next team meeting, ask your employees to share what they perceive to be the main barriers to their success. Ask follow-up questions like "How does what you shared impact you?" and "What ideas do you have to improve the situation?" Then pick at least one barrier to address. Commit to updating the team periodically, reporting progress in dismantling this barrier. This establishes your responsibility for creating an environment where your team can be successful, and it demonstrates that you are a Servant Leader.

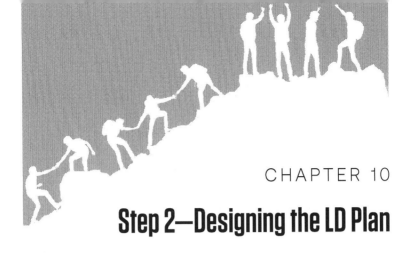

CHAPTER 10

Step 2—Designing the LD Plan

I remember the first LD program I attended. I had just been promoted to an Operations Leader for a manufacturing team that grew to one hundred twenty-five, with four direct-report Leaders and nine Leaders who reported to them. We were a team of fourteen leading the manufacturing floor.

This new opportunity carried with it an increased need for strategic, broad thinking, and for unifying a team of Leaders charged with starting up a manufacturing operation in a new location. We had a handful of experienced operators seeding the initial move. We were tasked with hiring the remainder of the new team. About six months into our start-up, I was given an opportunity to take a weeklong class on strategic Leadership at a prestigious university.

I found the program interesting, as we spent long days reading and discussing case studies, pouring over relevant trends, completing exercises, and presenting our work to the class. It was intellectually stimulating and motivational. And I had interesting information to take back to my team.

The only problem was that I returned to a hectic environment with tactical challenges sprouting everywhere: there were bugs to be worked out of production down equipment, we had unique defects to troubleshoot, the new team was still cutting their teeth and needing guidance, and as it was our annual performance-review period, everyone was scrambling to schedule time to support that process.

In such chaos, I had no chance to share what I had learned in my training! Moreover, it wasn't applicable to our current environment, nor was it aligned with the time of the year that strategic plans were due. I felt like I was trying to play chess while driving an Indy car. Ultimately, while what I had learned was interesting, it was many months before I could start thinking about applying it. By that time, both my enthusiasm and command of the material had waned; I ended up utilizing perhaps 10 percent of what I had learned.

I contrast this story with an educational event some months later. By then having worked out the bugs and we were starting to set up systems to manage the operation: meeting schedules, metric reviews, accountabilities, reporting, and the like. At that time, I and three other Leaders, whom I considered our core operations team, drove together to benchmark a similar manufacturing operation at a plant renowned for its operational excellence. We spent two days learning their culture of constructive feedback, seeing their product flow and how they measured and managed it, and attending stand-up meetings where they connected daily production status with weekly and monthly goals. And we observed their QCDSP metrics boards (Quality, Cost, Delivery, Safety, and People) and how each person reported on achievements, action items, and updates to commitments in previous meetings.

On the drive back, we discussed the operational relevance of what we had seen. And the next week, we began implementing 80 percent of it. It was useful, relevant, and exactly what we needed. Additionally, it wasn't one person bearing the burden of implementation but four of us partnering in the plan and its execution. This experience was the basis for what became an effective and efficient system to manage our operation, and the process of learning and defining it was aligning for our new team. The long-term implications of this trip were deeply positive.

Information must be crisply relevant to the environment, or it won't be applied. It's with a deep understanding of the unique challenges of the Leadership team that LD professionals need to teach targeted and applicable information to address specific, current needs. This enables maximum utilization of time and creates the highest probability for behavioral growth and impact.

> **Information must be crisply relevant to the environment, or it won't be applied.**

Typically, organizations either have created or have access to a wide variety of Leadership materials and tools. A broad-brush application of this content in a standard cohort training can miss the target for delivering timely content applicable to the environment of each student Leader. Additionally, interesting concepts evaporate into the ether when environmental circumstances limit time to apply them. Conversely, value is maximized when LD professionals teach materials relevant to addressing the current needs of their team.

In this step of HUM-B-LE, a team-specific plan is defined. LD professionals comb through the current state measurement data from the survey and the interviews in partnership with the team's Leader(s). This discussion identifies the biggest opportunities. A review of the data creates a list of needs, prioritizing this list, then defining objectives, which creates the charter for the LD team, who can then define a plan. The plan can include enrollment in existing training classes, application of existing tools and processes, or the creation of materials that don't currently exist. The point is that the need drives what the LD program delivers.

In the end, the LD professional and local Leaders agree to a plan and partner in its execution. Needs vary and understanding and targeting the specific needs of the team creates the greatest value for the trainer and customer.

Deliverable:

At the end of this step, the LD professional and the Leadership team have an agreed-upon plan for addressing top priorities of the team. This populates the "custom support" step of the HUM-B-LE process.

Chapter 10 Summary:

- In step 2, as a result of reviewing survey data, interviewing team members, and self-identification of team needs, the LD team makes plans for addressing all of the needs they have defined relative to growing the Leadership team.

- This step is in partnership with the Leadership team that agrees with what is determined as a timely development need for their team.

Practice:

As you look at your current personal situation, identify one development area that would help you the most to meet expectations now and near-term. Now determine a plan to grow in this area.

Step 3—Developing Individual and Team Emotional Intelligence

In defining emotional intelligence, as mentioned briefly in Chapter 5, we spotlight the five skills and include a fifth component:

1. **Self-Awareness:** the ability to be conscious of your own emotions.

2. **Self-Management:** the ability to leverage self-awareness to positively control your behavior.

3. **Other-Awareness:** the ability to accurately assess the emotions of others.

4. **Relationship Management:** the application of the first three components to create productive conversations and healthy relationships.

5. **Resilience:** the motivation to grow your E.I. E.I. can be both learned and lost, and this fifth component acknowledges the need to continue to practice growing E.I.

Some years ago, I led an operations team that included Leaders of both the engineering group and the manufacturing team. Helen, an engineering Leader, a very smart, insightful person, was deeply respected by the team. I directly led Helen's Leader, Michael. One day, in a meeting with about eight of us Leaders in a conference room, we were discussing a particularly challenging problem, and I was thinking ahead a bit as team members shared ideas. As my attention wandered, then returned to the meeting, one of the male Leaders shared an idea to which I responded that it made a lot of sense.

At that point, Michael said, "Well, Brett, Helen made that same suggestion about five minutes ago. Maybe it needed to come from a man for you to hear it?" Michael and I had a good relationship, and his tone was teasing but candid. Uncomfortably, I looked at Helen and asked, "Is that true?" She nodded.

Embarrassed by this revelation, I immediately apologized. I also acknowledged that while I was daydreaming a bit, maybe I also had unconscious bias that prevented me from hearing the suggestion coming from a woman. In any case, I took the opportunity to thank Michael for pointing out my slight, and I appreciated that he held me accountable. It also allowed me to acknowledge the value of everyone holding each other accountable, challenging each other appropriately.

Over the next couple of weeks, the team lit into me pretty good; whenever there was a valuable idea, they went out of their way to attribute it to Helen. Michael's observation not only resulted in my being more self-aware, but it also grew the collective team emotional intelligence, adding a spirit of playfulness. Ultimately, it helped make it safe to challenge each other.

If Michael hadn't called me on my insensitivity, Helen would have walked away frustrated. She probably would have judged my mistake as chauvinistic and perhaps shut down in future conversations. Further, others might have drawn similar conclusions. As a Leader, I could have just moved forward blind to my mistake, wondering why the team seemed disengaged. Michael's simple action allowed me to be conscious, to address the short-sightedness, to admit fault, and to promote independent thinking. This produced subsequent interactions that were engaging, creative, authentic, and even fun. This is the value of both individual and team emotional intelligence.

Multiple research sources have drawn the correlation between successful Leaders and high E.I.—maybe the most well-known being *Emotional Intelligence 2.0* by Travis Bradberry, PhD, and Joan Greaves, PhD, a book promoted by the Dalai Lama. E.I., they write, "accounts for 58% of performance . . . is the single biggest predictor of performance . . . and the strongest driver of leadership and personal excellence." But what is even better news than this, unlike I.Q., emotional intelligence (E.Q.) can be taught. Moreover, when not nurtured, E.I. can also be lost.

With this information, why do most LD programs not include E.I. as a centerpiece? For LD programs to move the needle on Leadership performance, E.I. must be a foundational component. This is why it is the staple of the HUM-B-LE method.

The HUM-B-LE approach goes one step beyond the teaching and growing of E.I.; additionally, we do it with a Leadership team that works closely together. This allows us to accomplish the following objectives with our E.I. class:

- Grow individual E.I.

- Grow team E.I.

- Create a relationship between team members where constructive challenge is not only safe but expected.

- Share vulnerability, perspectives, and experiences that deepen relationships.

- Grow the use of teammates as resources for coaching, role-playing, and feedback.

- Establish expectations for ongoing growth in this area.

- Practice and improve our ability as Leaders to both effectively give conversational feedback and receive feedback curiously.

- Teach basic coaching skills and the power of open-ended questions.

Key Components of the E.I. Class:

Vulnerability Exercise: When we begin the E.I. class, we set the stage for promoting vulnerability by having the most senior Leader receive unrehearsed feedback in front of the team. We use this to break down the fear of challenging the Leader. It illustrates how Leaders can create safety by the way they receive feedback. And we use it to demonstrate the power of curiosity and receptivity in learning. In preparation, we coach the Leader (before class) to respond with curiosity and ask questions to better understand the feedback. This enables us to highlight the benefits of how the Leader responded.

When a Leader focuses on understanding the feedback and asks questions to deeply understand it, that Leader demonstrates that it is safe to challenge.

Receiving Feedback in a Position of Authority: The previous exercise leads to a broader conversation of how Leaders can effectively receive feedback.

If you have ever given feedback to your Leader, I would guess that it was done only after weeks of contemplation, consideration of the potential outcomes, and rehearsing what to say. You likely lost sleep as you were deciding how much longer to remain silent and braced for the worst possible outcome. Ultimately, the pain of your Leader's behavior overcame your anxiety in giving feedback. Thus, in working through the discomfort, you were in fact providing a service to everyone involved.

As a Leader, viewing feedback as an act of service defuses the situation. Whether it is accurate or justified falls away when seeing this action as "caring for my wellbeing": *This person cared enough about me to work through great discomfort to show me how I can improve.* Additionally, when we realize that we all have blind spots and we need each other to help us identify ways to improve that we weren't aware of, this creates a healthy, authentic, and honest culture. Thus, it is important that we encourage these behaviors by welcoming feedback.

Being an engineer, I was predisposed to process all the data and determine the best path forward. When someone provided feedback about something that I did not agree with, I would share the information that justified my decision or behavior. I did not regard it as being difficult, just being accurate.

One example of this was when, in a performance review, I was too passionate. This led me to outline how my passion actually drove me to excel and that this, in turn, carried over to greater team success. Then one day after I'd just completed a conference call, working from home, my wife said, "You got your high voice again." I responded (in a high voice), "What are you talking about?" In reacting this way, I finally realized the wisdom in the feedback. You see, I had always regarded my passion as a positive, but my wife helped me to see that it caused me to get louder and higher in pitch. That might be intimidating, I could now understand; it might make me appear set in my ways—harder to work with. Moreover, as I justified my behavior in the face of feedback, it reinforced a similar message: that I was not safe to confront. I could finally see how my passion had been a barrier to collaboration. I needed to tone it down. This has been a focus of improvement for me ever since.

When a Leader sincerely desires to comprehend the feedback and asks questions to consider the perspective of the giver, it demonstrates that it's safe to be challenging. Even if a Leader's behavior is justified, focused listening and receiving is the only important thing in that moment. In the moment, *it is not about being right*. If Leaders can justify their behavior, we teach them to wait till some future point in time to share it. Any explanation at the time feedback is given will have a dismissive effect. It communicates that the employee providing input is *wrong*—which creates disincentive to speak up in the future. In the moment, the job of the Leader receiving feedback is to simply receive. You can always provide additional clarifications later: "Hey, remember two days ago when you gave me feedback on xxxx? Well, I was thinking about that and, by the way, I really appreciated you raising that issue with me. I was also wondering whether you were aware of xxxx."

Giving Feedback when in a Position of Authority: I had just taken a new Leadership role and was starting to get familiar with the new team. The front-line Leaders I led had a wide range of experiences and educational backgrounds, but all seemed smart, thoughtful, responsible, and well-spoken. In addition to getting to know the Leaders, I also set up meetings with small groups of operators to be able to meet with all two hundred manufacturing employees on the team. In these meetings, I felt a different vibe. Underneath the politeness, there was palpable frustration; it was as if they were evaluating me to see if I could be trusted with the truth. I would ask probing questions and receive a hesitant, watered-down answer that didn't quite line up with their body language.

Then I got a breakthrough. I met with a group of courageous operators who, five minutes into the meeting, just came out with it. They felt disrespected, as if they were being treated like children having to ask for permission to leave the line to go to the bathroom. They felt a small minority of "favorites" had good relationships with Leaders, but nobody trusted these teammates. Generally, the only time Leaders talked to them, they felt, was to accuse them of doing something wrong. Thereafter, I knew what to ask in these small team meetings. What I discovered was that this feeling of disrespect summed up the experience of a large percentage of the team.

So, what does a new Leader do with this information? If you go directly to the established Leaders, you create distrust between them and their team. You might also be thought to demonstrate that you will take negative information and draw conclusions from it, siding with operators closed to the Leaders' perspective. If you do nothing, you lose credibility with those who opened up to you. What I chose to do was to start having conversations with the Leaders about the challenges they were facing specifically around people issues and how they were handling them.

In one of these meetings, we were exploring how to give feedback effectively. I suggested conversational feedback whereby the Leader outlines an observable set of facts, asking for the perspective of the recipient of the feedback. It goes something like this:

"Hey, Bill, I was reviewing the rejects from yesterday and noticed that six of the eight came from the processes that you were running. Were you aware of this? What were the issues that you were facing yesterday? What do you think we should do differently?"

The objective is for Bill to acknowledge the existence of the facts, to take ownership, and to engage in problem-solving. If Bill's performance was at the root of the issue and he owns up to it, the Leader will just be supportive in helping Bill improve. If Bill's actions were at the root of the issue and he *isn't* owning his responsibility, the Leader will be more direct about performance expectations. In the end, they agree to a plan moving forward.

As I broached this topic, one of the Leaders objected, "Well, sometimes you need to be proactive, in the moment. For example, if the person walks in five minutes late to work, I need to say, 'Hey, you're five minutes late; that isn't acceptable because your team is counting on you to help them meet the build plan.'"

I remember thinking, *Now I get it!* To me this was a very clear, conscientious reaction that for a manager seemed reasonable, but not for a Leader.

So, I asked about how operators felt about this message: "Would you argue or just go to work? What if the employee had a good reason to be late? How would you feel as an operator if you had just paused to help an upset teammate, and that was your reason for being late? Would you explain or just put your head down and go back to work, frustrated by being chastised for doing the right thing? How would you feel as a Leader, having given this feedback without asking for the late employee's perspective, then eventually finding out the reason for their lateness?"

I have personally had numerous experiences that necessitated surgeries to remove my foot from my mouth. Feedback without curiosity often results in exposing false assumptions—that is, if you are lucky; sometimes people just take it and don't engage in explaining the circumstance. My personal history of reacting in this fashion taught me to engage with curiosity.

The fact of the matter is that if done right, feedback situations are opportunities to address concerns together; to learn about situations, to understand perspectives, and to develop a lasting sense of personal responsibility. These interactions call for assumptions of good intentions. You are trying to understand what seems to be suboptimal behavior, assuming employees are doing their absolute best. This method starts with stating the facts of the situation, then asking for the other's perspective.

We teach the value of conversational feedback. If the purpose of feedback is to enable a behavior change, it is best to help the receiver identify the need to improve instead of just flatly stating it. When Leaders give feedback using the common practice of Situation, Behavior, Impact (SBI), they state the facts of the behavior and how it impacts the employee and/or the team. This common technique may make for a clear communication of a need to change; however, it is a one-way message that creates frustration and promotes subordination. It does not demonstrate an assumption of positive intent, and it often feels disrespectful.

Therefore, we teach a modified version of SBI: Situation, Behavior, Ask (SBA). Differently from SBI, in SBA, the Leader engages the follower in a conversation requiring feedback. Stating observable facts and asking for the receiver's perspective, the Leader creates a conversation about the behavior, which triggers personal ownership. And ownership is key to lasting behavior change.

Example from above using SBI Feedback:

"As you know, we have an aggressive build plan this month (situation). This morning, you were five minutes late to your workstation (behavior). When you are late, it lets down your team and makes it harder for us to meet our goals (impact).

Using SBA Feedback:

"As you know, we have an aggressive build plan this month (situation). This morning, you were five minutes late to your workstation (behavior). *Is everything okay (ask)? What happened?*

This approach allows employees to explain what caused their lateness. Possible outcomes:

1. If they have a valid reason, they are invited to share it. They experience their Leader treating them respectfully, with concern and curiosity.

2. If they were at fault—and lack a good explanation—they will most likely take personal responsibility: "Yeah, I screwed up and hit the snooze button too many times." In this case, the Leader can ask for a plan to avoid this in the future; personal responsibility has been established.

3. If they are at fault and don't take personal responsibility, the Leader can now be firmer. Employee: "There is nothing I could do; the traffic was bad this morning." Leader: "Yes, sometimes traffic is bad, but it is still your responsibility and nobody else's for you to be on time. So, how are you

going to ensure you are on time even when traffic is heavy?"

Role-Playing: In E.I. class, we practice giving and receiving conversational feedback through role-playing. This begins before class by understanding common conflicts that occur in the specific environment of attendees. I then create relevant, real-world role-play situations. For that, we assign the roles of initiator, receiver, and observer. After they talk through what happened in the role-play, they discuss what went well and what could have been better, with each member of the role-play offering observations. Then these three-person teams come back to the class to share their learning. We do this three times, so that each person gets an opportunity to play each role. Effective feedback conversations take practice, but it is one of the most important skills to have as an effective Leader.

Answering the "Why" of E.I.: We define the components of E.I. and share research that details the value of growing it. We have a conversation that invites contrasting opinions of its value. In this conversation, we attempt to deepen our view of the importance of E.I. to an effective Leader.

The Inner Critic:

We talk about the "inner critic" voice that we all have, and the need to be conscious of it in order to gain control of its potentially negative influence. We discuss the value of not judging anyone—ourselves or others—as judging clouds curiosity and true learning. We can judge acts but not each other. This is a key aspect of the class, as most students are aware of their "inner critic," but few have questioned its impact or been conscious of its bias in negativity that holds us back. Yet, we have tools to negate its one-sided view of the world. We can diminish its negative influence and it starts with awareness. Then we use the tools of mindfulness practices that I cover later in the chapter.

Attitude:

Pause for a moment to consider two different people. First, think about someone you dread being around and try to avoid. Let's call him Jonny. When you see this person, you try not to make eye contact; if he engages, you think of some excuse as to why you can't talk. Now consider Diana, whose effect on you is the opposite. She's the first you invite to a party, someone you track down to talk to, and you deeply enjoy her presence.

Typically, what makes these two people different is their attitude. Jonny is negative; it's all about him; the world is set up to make his life hard. He tries to pull you into his cynicism, looking for someone to validate his explanation for struggling. Conversations with the complainers of the world suck out your energy and leave you exhausted. Conversely, Diana is upbeat, positive, a good listener who is interested in you and sees possibility in everything. She is optimistic, upbeat, and you feel energized in her presence. Jonny and Diana's attitudes are very different.

Attitude, unlike personality, we can control. In the E.I. class, we discuss Bruce D. Schneider's Energy Leadership™ Index, which, he says in his Brain Basics website description, "will elaborate on how your energy shows up while experiencing a typical day and what happens to your energy when you perceive a stressful situation." This model facilitates a deeper consciousness of our attitude and, thereby, an ability to choose a "higher" attitude that serves us and our team, our significant other, and our family better. See **Appendix 2** for a list of the levels of attitude in the Energy Leadership Index.

Coaching:

We perform a simple coaching exercise where after we pair off, one person shares a challenging struggle; the other (the coach) is allowed to respond in only three ways:

- Ask open-ended questions to examine the challenge deeper.
- Reflectively listen to verify you understand the challenge.
- Affirm the challenge such as by saying, "I totally understand; anyone in your situation would have similar emotions."

While this is a simple exercise, insufficient for teaching how to be a coach, it helps grow the skill of asking open-ended questions, which, in turn, helps people consider for themselves their reaction, becoming more mentally engaged. Where yes/ no questions create narrowness in response, open-ended questions are expansive, inviting the responders to broaden their reflections. For example, "Are you feeling frustrated?" is limiting. "How are you feeling?" is expansive and invites you to connect with your emotions and share your truth.

Mindfulness:

To demonstrate the power mindfulness has to reveal wisdom, reset our emotions, and facilitate growth (see **Appendix 2** for a list of mindfulness techniques), we practice it both in and outside (as homework) of class. Much literature exists about the power of mindfulness, so I will leave it to other works to detail its value. However, in my experience, about 50 percent of the Leaders I teach have limited knowledge of or experience with mindfulness techniques; a much larger number do not engage in a regular practice. This is an area of great opportunity.

I view mindfulness as similar to rebooting a computer. When you have left your computer on for a week or more, it commonly starts to operate less efficiently and may even have difficulty running some programs. Often this can be reconciled by rebooting it. Similarly, when people are constantly "on," jumping from one task to the next, their mind furiously active, they tend to get worn down and lose their ability to effectively regulate their behavior. Tasks start to run them; they do not thoughtfully determine their next action. A daily mindfulness practice helps "reboot" your emotions, get you centered, and navigate relationships successfully.

Other: There are other modules we might use in the class, which we include or omit based on what is most pertinent to the needs of the team. Other modules include:

- Personality assessments (from various sources).
- Psychological Safety: how to grow it in your team.
- Self-Determination Theory (autonomy, relatedness, and mastery) and how Leaders can provide this for their team.

- The value of humility in a Leader, approached through the lens of Jim Collins's *Good to Great* (4,000,000 copies sold).

- The value of trust as detailed in the *New York Times* and # 1 *Wall Street Journal* bestselling book *The Speed of Trust*, by Steven M. R. Covey

The E.I. class takes place over multiple days, which enables homework exercises and personal reflection between classes to seed an ongoing mindfulness practice. Most participants have never experienced this type of training in their career and are deeply grateful for the nonjudgmental insight into their thought process. And going through this together provides comfort in knowing that they're not alone; that we share similar fears, insecurities, and emotions as we strive to be successful Leaders.

Growing E.I. isn't learned in school; it often requires changing our perspective. But the fact that we go through the teaching together is both empowering and inspirational.

It's important to acknowledge the ability to lose E.I. so that we're deliberate in our ongoing practice of its skills. Bradberry and Greaves share data detailing a drop-off in the average levels of E.I. as Leaders advance from mid-managers through directors and executives up to CEO. While they don't analyze the reasons behind this, I would speculate several potential explanations:

- Growing E.I. involves some level of feedback, and the "higher" the Leader, the more difficult it is to speak truth to power.

- E.I. requires making the effort to be conscious of the self, to regulate the self, to be conscious of others' emotions, and to manage relationships. Potentially, the busier the person is, the less time for practicing E.I.

- Broad Leaders' actions may be insulated from their effects. This distance may reduce feedback, when contrasted with what front-line Leaders experience in sitting with and seeing the impact on their team.

- In making difficult decisions, Broad Leaders may feel overwhelmed by responsibility, motivating them to not get "too close" to those impacted.

- With Broad Leaders the emphasis may come down heavily on the side of doing. Mindfulness and growing E.I. require reflection. These Leaders may not see enough value to invest the time in it.

I recommend reading *Emotional Intelligence 2.0*, which has a list of recommended practices on how to grow in the first four dimensions of E.I. More than just a book defining the value of E.I., it is also a practical guide outlining helpful practices for how to grow this competence.

> Going through E.I. training together provides comfort in knowing that we share similar fears and insecurities.

Deliverable:

E.I. has been augmented individually and as a team. The team members have learned more about themselves and their teammates, and they have grown together accordingly. They have concepts, terminology, and motivation to evolve their own E.I. and to help each other on this journey.

Chapter 11 Summary:

- Emotional intelligence is the single most important attribute correlated with success as a Leader.

- E.I. can be taught and grown with practice as well as diminished without.

- There's both personal E.I. and team E.I., which enables a team to work more effectively together.

- This chapter also listed the topics for teaching E.I. that the HUM-B-LE development process covers.

Practice:

Do you demonstrate a high level of emotional intelligence as a Leader? I have created an assessment to help you answer this question. You will also receive tips on how to grow your Leadership E.I. Simply **scan** on the QR code below.

Step 4—Addressing Custom Team Needs

In Step 2 of the HUM-B-LE approach, we detailed how to design a plan to address the specific developmental needs of the Leadership team. In Step 4 that plan is executed. Of the opportunities we identified, some can be addressed with existing institutional training, tools, and/or processes. In that case, you can simply connect the identified need with existing training and support resources (internal and external). For example:

Identified Need	Existing Resource
Grow problem-solving skills	Continuous Improvement Program
Write Performance Reviews	YouTube Class
Create a Diverse, Inclusive Workplace	DEI Training through HR
Grow new Leader success	Leader Onboarding Program

The point of this step is that *pushing* training onto teams is less impactful than addressing an identified team need. The need gives the training relevance, creates a "pull" and a receptivity—helping ensure commitment. If a self-identified need doesn't align cleanly with an already existing resource, the LD team figures out how to meet the custom need. For example, with the item "Grow new Leader success," if there is no current Leader-onboarding program, the LD professional should work with existing Leaders to set up an onboarding process. Likely as not, many existing Leaders or HR professionals already have checklists they use to onboard new Leaders. In that case, the LD professional might simply bring these sources together to create a consistent approach to new-Leader onboarding.

In another example, let's say that data in the measurement step revealed significantly less trust of Leadership on one specific team. In Step 4, the LD professional could work with the specific Leader to understand the situation better (possibly a 360-degree review), coaching the Leader in how to build trust, or providing additional training pertinent to the Leader's growth needs in this area. This might require supporting an individual Leader's needs for focused assistance that data reveals.

Here is a recent example. When I was working with a team, our review of its environment identified that Leaders there too often interceded to address interpersonal issues between employees. Employee A would come to the Leader to complain about employee B. Then typically the Leader jumped in to resolve the problem either by facilitating a conversation, giving feedback to employee B, or involving HR. We discussed the potential destructive effect of these actions in undermining the relationship between employees A and B.

Employee B would typically resent that A had gone to their Leader and had not come to them.

We reviewed this challenge, and the Leadership team acknowledged that their actions undermined the ability for teammates to have relationships of mutual respect. Also, the Leaders complained that employees were bringing relationship frustrations to them on a daily basis.

After talking about the need to teach/coach employees to communicate directly with each other, we came up with a plan. The team would identify why it was important for employees to be respectfully direct with each other. Then Leaders would be trained on how to teach feedback skills. Next, the intention to move in this direction and share the "why" would be presented to the broad team. And finally, with this behavior added to performance expectations, employees would be trained in the necessary skills. My role as an LD professional then became that of a training facilitator in support of the culture initiative that was owned by the Leadership team. They had a need specific to their environment, and we worked together to identify how to best meet it.

Deliverable:

In Step 4, the LD professional focuses on the specific custom needs the team has identified or that have bubbled up from the data. This support may include connecting the team or individual Leaders with existing, standard training. Creating a custom solution is at the other end of the spectrum. The point is to deliver a solution to the team to address their specific needs and avoid pushing training upon them that is of limited value.

Chapter 12 Summary:

For development needs that don't closely align with the standard LD steps in HUM-B-LE, find opportunities to utilize existing training resources. If none exist, the LD team should create the custom solutions.

Practice:

What one area do you think is the best opportunity to either grow as a Leader, or grow your ability to influence others. With that identified, consider the resources that already exist within your company, on the intranet, in your community, and choose to utilize one of these to grow your skills. Do it today.

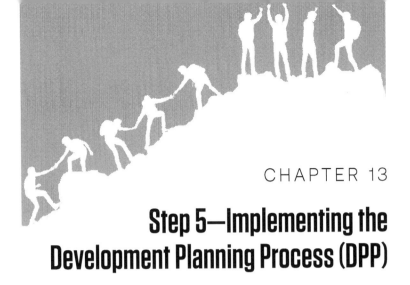

Step 5—Implementing the Development Planning Process (DPP)

I n the introduction, I shared my disastrous first leadership experience, where in ignorance I wasted time and alienated my team. Even though I tried to make up for my initial missteps, I probably never fully rebuilt the trust I lost. So, how do we avoid this situation and the distraction it created? The answer is through organizational processes to help prepare future Leaders prior to thrusting them into the role. If Leaders aren't actively preparing future Leaders, then those novice Leaders will likely experience numerous missteps that have a detrimental effect on the culture, as I did.

If you are a Leader, are you putting consistent, appropriate time into considering the training and preparation of future Leaders? Do you have a process for this? As new Leaders first make their commitment, are you actively gathering the perspectives of others and directing feedback and guidance back to them to help them grow their abilities? If these systems are lacking or are uneven across teams, then implementing the Development Planning Process (DPP) will address this need.

In the world of training and development, there is an accepted theory: the 70-20-10 model of learning. This model postulates that 70 percent of learning comes from experience, 20 percent comes from interactions with knowledgeable people, and 10 percent from classroom learning. Working with a nonprofit educational institution, Morgan McCall, Michael M. Lombardo, and Robert A. Eichinger created this breakdown in the 1980s. On this basis, it follows that the person best able to support an employee's learning should have the most knowledge of appropriate experiential opportunities. This will most commonly be their current Leader.

It is typically an expectation that Leaders develop future Leaders. Yet given the grind of meeting personal and team business objectives, this role often gets neglected—in which case succession planning suffers and new Leaders are ill prepared to step into their new position.

The importance of experience to a person's development suggests that Leaders should play a primary role in the development of existing and future Leaders. Except as a complementary element of the plan, this role should not be outsourced. In Step 5 of HUM-B-LE, we address the need for equipping Leaders with the tools and the process to regularly and consistently support the development of other Leaders. We call this the **Development Planning Process (DPP).**

> Leaders often get so tied up in the grind of meeting their personal and team's business objectives that developing successors gets neglected.

The DPP is a set of consistent steps that individuals or teams follow to identify opportunities for any employee who has expressed interest in growing as a

Leader. This could be both employees with no Leadership experience looking for an entry level role or, equally likely, current Leaders looking to grow into broader Leadership roles. Processes like these aren't novel, but the following attributes— sometimes missed—provide benefits beyond simply growing skills.

- Transparency: Share the program with everyone in the company. This has multiple benefits. It demonstrates the organization is committed to developing future Leaders. It takes developing Leaders out of the back room and makes it visible. And transparency builds trust and inclusion.

- Inclusiveness: With communication of the program comes an invitation for anyone who is interested to participate. This sends a message that the organization backs up the talk with behavior. Welcoming anyone who is interested dispels the potential criticism that the LD program plays favorites. Moreover, as Marcus Buckingham and Ashley Goodall detail in Chapter 7 of *Nine Lies About Work: A Freethinking Leader's Guide to the Real World*, potential in others is not easily predicted. People surprise us, and to think that we can predict potential is a mistake. Some of the best Leaders are those quietly competent employees whose capability as a Leader may not be obvious. In fact, the attribute of humility, which is highlighted in Chapter 1, is often hard to identify. If there is concern that an open invitation to support anyone interested in being a Leader will be impractical—that too many people will step up—it is my experience that an open invitation hasn't created those issues but rather has been manageable. Yet it sends the message that Leaders are not just handpicking favorites for future promotion.

- Diversity: The LD program should monitor the diversity of all the aspiring candidates; if they don't represent the overall diversity of the population, the organization should proactively address this inconsistency. For example, if 20 percent of your developees are people of color and the broader population is 50 percent, the gap is extreme and should be addressed. One way is to identify and encourage diverse candidates who may not have considered Leadership in the past. Ultimately, the best way to have a diverse Leadership team is to create a diverse pool of developees and grow them. This enables diverse choice when openings become available and should be a stated goal for the program.

- Consistency of Assessment: Create a consistent methodology to assess the readiness of individual developees for promotion. This breeds fairness and enables comparison across teams, with the ability to roll up data. However, don't rely on a detailed list of specific competencies. It is my belief that these categories should be broad enough to illustrate that competence in each area is necessary for promotion. Categories such as "people skills" and "hard skills" are examples of attributes that are necessary for Leadership success.

- Keep it Simple, Based in Values: In determining these broad categories, be sure they align with

DISCOVERING LEADERS WITHIN

company values. This ensures Leaders are developed in alignment with the foundational principles of the organization. Additionally, I recommend utilizing a small number of broad categories of competence that most can agree are necessary for Leader success. Do not have any more than four to seven, or the assessment can become overly complex and expectations are watered down.

- Include Strength Development: Research concludes that leveraging strengths yields significantly greater business value than focusing on weaknesses. When we define four to seven key performance categories, we hone in on the biggest priorities for a developee while also identifying strengths and discussing how these can be leveraged.

The determination of broad areas for assessing Leaders' development opportunities is an important subject of discussion. The areas chosen should reflect the values of the organization (e.g., people leading versus asset management, long-term thinking versus short-term financial performance, collaboration versus hierarchy). They also need to be relevant to the functional area the Leader is assigned (expectations in Leading manufacturing may be different than in Leading accounting or sales). To capture key areas, they should be the right mix yet still be simple and easy to remember.

> **The determination of broad areas for assessing Leaders' development should reflect the values of the organization.**

We determined, within a manufacturing environment, the foundational importance of a Leader having six primary competencies. These were used to assess each developee, characterizing each individual in every area into one of three categories: 1. Still developing, 2. Competent, or 3. Area of strength. Below are the six categories we assessed:

- **Hard Skills:** An ability to understand and manage manufacturing theory, metrics, planning processes, and overall complexity called for in their role. This includes project management, problem-solving, financial acumen, etc.

- **People Skills:** An ability to communicate effectively, including being proficient in giving and receiving feedback, creating engagement, influencing coworkers, and creating ownership in their team; i.e., the ability to coach, to have difficult conversations, and to build natural followership independent of title.

- **Experience:** Relevant experience, which reveals whether they are ready for promotion. Here we consider length in role, diversity of experience, size of team, complexity of supply chain, external experiences, education, etc. Additionally, consider whether the person has had sufficient time in a role to have initiated, completed, and been held accountable for the success of initiatives put forward.

- **Personal Growth and Track Record Growing Others:** Make sure the individual has a history in both personal development and developing others. Attention to advancing your own skills and a commitment to supporting others is critical to long-term success as a Leader. This is relevant if your company value is that employees should always be advancing their skills and supporting each other's growth.

- **Reliability and Initiative:** This means a track record of doing what you say and meeting your goals. Does this developee consistently meet commitments and overcome barriers? Also, consistently look for the next area to improve and step up to help teammates?

- **Preparation for the Next Step:** What is the developee's knowledge of the role being sought? Has the developee performed any of it or shadowed someone in the role? Can the employee step in when their Leader is absent? Having a base level of familiarity in this area enables the developee to know whether the next role is of personal interest and to be able to be successful in a shorter period of time after a promotion.

With this assessment process and consistent categories, the workforce planning improves. Now you have a list of people who are "ready now," "ready in one to two years," or "developing" with respect to the Leadership role they're targeting. In this way the organization can understand bench strength, address common themes for development, and inform a hiring strategy. Moreover, it enables Leaders to identify strengths that may be best tailored to one opening in particular. Finally, the data identifies development themes where additional training could benefit the greatest number of people.

L. BRETT LARSON

When assessing developees, keep a team perspective: This is not a process where an individual Leader assesses an individual developee. We all have biases and blind spots, and research shows that when we assess others, unfortunately, instead of seeing them as *they* are, we see them as *we* are. More often, evaluations are an indication of the assessor rather than of the assessed.

Evaluations improve and biases dwindle when multiple perspectives are brought in and team members productively challenge each other during the assessment conversation. Thus, have readiness assessments done by a team of non-peer Leaders knowledgeable about the developee. For example, an Operations Leader, Technical Leader, and Human Resources Generalist can together assess a manufacturing Leader who is developing into an Operations Leader. When multiple voices with different perspectives share their observations, a three-dimensional view is possible and the conversation is a rich, informed discussion. An additional benefit is that the entire team of assessors is then familiar with the development path of the developee and can take part in supporting their growth.

> We all have biases and blind spots . . . thus readiness assessments should be done by a team . . . knowledgeable about the developee.

Now let's look at the sequential steps in the process. In outlining the process, let's consider "Broad Leaders" of a couple of teams (I and II) who are supporting the development of "Leaders of Leaders" (A and B) in an operation where they lead

104

other "Front-line Leaders" (1, 2, and 3) per the organizational chart below.

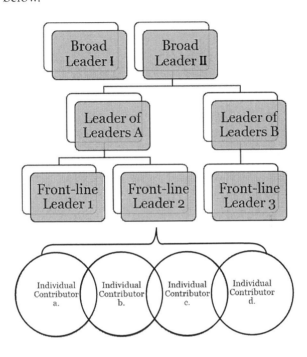

Development Planning Process Steps:

1. Let's assume we're supporting the development of the Front-Line Leader 1, Sam, into a Leader of Leaders role. Leader of Leaders A, Barney, gathers historical information on developees interested in growing into the next-level Leadership role. Information Barney gathers includes records of experience and accomplishments, recent development, strength of followership, technical skills, and other relevant

performance information for assessing Sam against the readiness criteria.

2. Leader of Leaders A (Barney) calls a Development Planning Process (DPP) meeting to discuss the developees and invites Broad Leader II (and possibly Broad Leader I), Leader of Leaders B, and others, such as HR and an informed Technical Leader. At the meeting, this team first assesses each developee against the predetermined criteria. The team discusses each person and determines for each broad category whether the person is "still developing," "competent," or if this is a "significant strength." For any attribute that's "still developing" or a "significant strength," the group details the reason behind their characterization. The output then becomes a list of what each developee needs to grow and a list of their strengths to leverage.

3. The team identifies one or two specific actions that will either support development in areas of gaps, utilize strengths, or both. And they document any recent development items the developee has completed.

4. The team then decides which person will provide feedback to each developee outside of the meeting on the readiness assessment and the actions from Step 3. This conversation ensures the developee knows how to grow into the "next level," and how others perceive their readiness.

5. In the same meeting, following steps 1–4, the team continues to discuss additional developees in the same manner until everyone has been considered.

6. Future meetings are scheduled (we recommend quarterly) to repeat the steps and continue to support developee growth. In future meetings, simply update the readiness categories if changes in competence have occurred. These meetings are much shorter.

The second part of the DPP involves broadly communicating how the process works and how it's leveraged for organizational benefit. This information is shared with the extended team, and it removes Leadership Development from being a "back-room" hidden process—making it transparent to everyone.

1. After communicating the existence of the DPP to their organization, the Broad Leader invites anyone interested in developing as a Leader to participate.
2. The Broad Leader, being ultimately responsible for the administration and support of the DPP, can and should also use this process to set goals. This includes goals for improving the diversity of the group of developees and growing the number of "ready now" Leaders.

The DPP enables an organization to not just talk about the value of diversity, but to actively grow it. This approach *does not limit anyone* but creates choice, including options for selecting from qualified developees in the underrepresented populations.

I have used this process effectively with the following scenario. In 2018, my team started to

> . . . a more diverse group of developees . . . ultimately . . . grows a more diverse Leadership team.

proactively encourage an underrepresented ethnic group. This group made up approximately 26 percent of the company's overall manufacturing population. Only 3 percent of my team's leaders and 6 percent of our developees represented this group. Our team then identified individuals from the underrepresented team who, we felt, had high Leadership potential. We then reached out to these individuals, encouraging them to be future Leaders and let us support their development. Employing this process, we were able to identify six new developees from this underrepresented group. Within two years, five of the six were Leaders. With proactive efforts, simply by committing to greater diversity in developees, we grew the number of Leaders representing this group from 3 percent to 20 percent. And each one of them was successful as a new Leader. Finally, this previously underrepresented population now had role models encouraging their own development efforts.

On the topic of Diversity, Equity and Inclusion (DEI), **Appendix 2** lists additional approaches to growing DEI within your organization.

Deliverable:

At the end of this step, the Leadership team is executing the Development Planning Process whereby they assess developing Leaders, identify learning and development opportunities for each individual, and begin conversations with them about these opportunities. You can also use this process to demonstrate inclusiveness by inviting any interested party to participate. Moreover, it creates proactive diversity in the group of developees. The DPP helps create a culture of learning and eventually a deep, diverse bench of future Leaders.

Chapter 13 Summary:

- Leaders should be actively developing future Leaders as a part of their commitment. The Development Planning Process is a standard approach for identifying opportunities and facilitating development conversations.

- When Leaders follow a consistent approach, it enables an inclusive and fair process that creates a culture of growth and learning.

- Broad categories for assessing Leaders' development needs should be defined as a reflection of the values of the organization and what is expected of their Leaders.

- Assessments that include multiple members of the Leadership team reduce the potential for bias and create richer conversations that enable a team to collaborate on how to support individuals. This also provides richer feedback to developees.

- Having a consistent LD process like DPP also creates the ability to be inclusive and transparent, and grow increased diversity.

Practice:

Reflect on areas where your organization lacks diversity. By what processes do you promote employees? Where are there biases in the process that need to be addressed? How can you create additional opportunities that help feed the process with more diverse candidates?

CHAPTER 14

Step 6—Creating a Sustainment Plan

T en years into my career, I took a benchmarking trip to O.C. Tanner, a Salt Lake City-based company renowned for their culture and employee-recognition program. At their facility, we took a tour, and with each manufacturing cell we visited, the employees showed us their highly efficient processes, their suggestion and recognition boards, and the status of training of each employee. Besides showing us family pictures, they recounted personal success stories. They likewise talked about projects that were in process, how they reached out to partner with suppliers, and their inspirational interactions with customers.

Their deep sense of pride and ownership in their work was palpable. Moreover, their activities aligned with the company vision of "We help organizations appreciate people who do great work." They obviously lived that motto internally. For me that trip was eye-opening to the kind of culture that is possible when Leaders deeply value their employees.

Inspired by that visit, wanting to re-create a similar culture, I began striving to notice good works by my team on a more regular basis. So, I created a reminder on my calendar for an end-of-the-week review to reflect on the positive contributions I'd witnessed. This led me to start writing short notes to people on my team in recognition of their good work. This, in turn, created an improved relationship between me and my team, with many commenting on how much they appreciated the recognition.

As time passed and other priorities crept in, my enthusiasm waned. I started to skip using this reminder here and there. Then the reminder ran out, and I didn't even notice it. Sometime later, my Leader sent out an advocate to collect opinions of me; one of the comments was in gratitude that I'd written a card, expressing my appreciation. As I rehashed this with my Leader, I asked myself a poignant question: why had I forgotten to write such cards, and how was I going to renew the practice and make it stick? Obviously, a reminder on my calendar hadn't been enough.

I recommitted my efforts by taking several steps:

1. I put the goal of recognition of others into my development plan, to be assessed in my annual performance review.

2. I added an agenda to our weekly Leadership meeting to identify where each of us had recognized employees in the last week. This created peer support for performing these small acts of kindness and encouraged others to do the same.

3. In this meeting we used our plant's employee-recognition system and filled out thank-you notes to post on the recognition board. This made public our efforts to recognize individuals and demonstrated the Leadership team valued recognition.

Whenever we implement something, we must also consider how to sustain it in the long run—which I had not sufficiently planned for when I initially returned from OC Tanner.

In a study by David Coates entitled "Integrated Leadership Development Programmes: Are they Effective and What Role Does Coaching Play?" he documents challenges to sustaining learning. The study detailed that while 62 percent of students in an LD program applied what they learned right away, only 34 percent reported that they still, after one year, continued with the application.

The study contrasts this failure with the success of a second cohort class of Leaders. In this second cohort class, for the first year after completing the training, they received coaching support to apply the learning from the LD program. Coaching was utilized for one year post class. The study repeated the questions, this time two years after the LD training had ended and one year after coaching terminated. It found that the percentage of those who responded that they were still applying what they had learned was a whopping 96 percent. Whether coaching is required is unclear, but it can be concluded that some form of sustainment plan is important. In this step of HUM-B-LE, the LD profession facilitates a sustainment-planning process to help the Leadership team define activities for retaining and consistently practicing what they've learned.

The key components suggested for this step are:

1. Review what Leaders learned in the HUM-B-LE development process.
    -   Examples: the power of effective feedback; the power of open-ended questions; mindfulness practices, the importance of a positive attitude; the importance of Leaders actively developing future Leaders, etc.

2. Identify where Leaders have already taken a new approach and which topics or tools they found most relevant.

    -   Examples: "I'm now taking time to set intentions at the start of every day." "Judy and I have been coaching each other every week, and that has helped me see a bigger picture." "Every day, I've been using mindfulness to notice two things I can appreciate in my teammates." "At the end of each of my meetings, I go around the table and ask for each person to share what the decisions made in the meeting mean to them."

3. Select two or three activities that—across the group of Leaders—are most common and valued as effective tools to retain growth.

    -   Examples: **1.** We pair up and coach each other for thirty minutes each week, alternating who is the coach and who is the client. **2.** In our weekly metric review, we add a standard agenda item in which each person selects someone to give positive recognition to. **3.** All Leaders add a daily reflection to their standard work (a document for the purpose of creating daily consistency in each Leader). **4.** We rotate teammates who will lead a monthly discussion of an E.I. topic or practice. **5.** Every six months we repeat the team survey and review the results together.

4. Finally, determine how to make sure these practices are embedded in habit. If the activity can be included in an existing process or regular meeting, it

is more likely to be sustained than if something new is created.

- From the list above, item 2 adds on to an existing meeting. Item 1 is a new commitment between each pair of Leaders, but if they already meet weekly, the meeting could just be extended to incorporate the coaching. Item 3 leverages an existing tool/process. Items 4 and 5 are probably a new event.

5. For each long-term activity that is identified, commit to a plan and the timeframe, and decide who is responsible for ensuring it gets followed.

For a brainstormed list of potential sustainment ideas, browse through **Appendix 2**.

Deliverable:

The team has defined a plan for how to incorporate some of the most valuable new concepts from training into their standard, habitual work.

Chapter 14 Summary:

- Based on the concepts the Leadership team has found most beneficial and applicable for the future, the LD professional facilitates the development of a sustainment plan.

- To make the number of sustainment activities manageable, I recommend two to three. It's better to be consistent with a few practices than to not sustain them because there are too many.

- Whenever possible, incorporate sustainment activities into existing meetings or processes.

Practice:

Consider something you learned in the past that you found valuable but, for whatever reason, are no longer utilizing it. Why were you unable to continue it? What could you do differently to make it a habit in the future?

CHAPTER 15

Step 7—Measure Future State

"Accountability" is a term often used in business, but in my experience its practice routinely falls short. One reason is that leaders think accountability is something a person in authority employs with a subordinate. My view is that accountability is a two-way street. It only works when we hold *each other* accountable.

In 2003, I took a job as a Manufacturing Leader at a company that was renowned for its culture. While my title stated I was a Leader, the company defined a Leader as someone who had followers. Being new, I had not yet earned followers.

Early on, I noticed inefficiencies in the flow of material in production. So, I started talking to operators and front-line Leaders who reported to me—giving them suggestions about rearranging the line to better connect the starting process (located in a separate room) with the process it fed. They looked at me like I was some kind of alien—*How do you know what's better? You haven't been here long enough, and we don't know you.* I quickly realized I was not yet their Leader, as I had not earned their followership.

Over the course of the next six months, I made it a point to be accountable to them. I started to listen to their frustrations and improvement ideas. These things became my priority as I worked to reduce the angst the issues they brought to my attention caused them. And I spent hours on the line, educating myself about what made their jobs hard. Over time, my focus won their respect. When I reintroduced the opportunity to rearrange the flow of the line to improve efficiencies months later, they began to participate in the conversation, identifying how to best implement the change. Ultimately, this improvement led to a 10 percent increase in efficiency, and my ability to effectively hold my team accountable was enabled because I was receptive to their holding me accountable.

Accountability is a two-way street, and while hierarchical managers, just because of their position, may have success in implementing change, they will not grow engagement and ownership unless they are also willing to be held accountable by their team.

This same principle is true when I am working to develop Leaders in the HUM-B-LE development process. Leadership teams hold me accountable for focusing on their needs and delivering helpful content. They give feedback on my effectiveness in delivering content and challenge me to provide evidence of the value of what I teach. They, in turn, I hold accountable for learning, evolving their approach to Leadership, and committing to improving the engagement of their teams. And together we own the goal of improving team survey scores.

In Steps 1 and 2, I defined a survey process, noting how it led to identifying LD opportunities. In this step, I, the LD professional and local Leaders share accountability for achieving improved survey results.

In the HUM-B-LE approach to LD, the objective is to improve Leaders' ability to lead in order to create a culture of engagement and psychological safety. At the onset, we measured the current state of these cultural attributes because research has isolated these two factors as key to driving high-performing teams and achieving superior business results. The challenge is that with so many other factors having direct bearing—market, societal, social, political, environmental, etc.—it's difficult to isolate just the LD impact on business performance. While this is true, evaluating the experience of the team being led, their engagement, and their feelings of safety is less confounded with other variables. These attributes are also largely determined by the conduct of the Leader.

> **Companies need to be clear on the objectives of their LD program and be accountable for improvement.**

Execution of the HUM-B-LE development program creates improved behaviors in Leaders. Yet, after Leaders have grown their E.I. and adjusted their approach, it still takes time for employees to experience the change and gain confidence that it will last. Depending on the magnitude of the Leader's change, I believe the right amount of time to pass before measuring the future state should be three-to-six months after completing the sustainment plan. Since this survey duplicates the "current state measurements" executed in Step 1 (measuring engagement and PS in the broad team), it provides a direct comparison between employees' experiences before/after the LD program.

The LD professional feels accountable for growing Leaders to the point where those they lead have an improved experience at work. The local Leadership Team feels accountable for generating improved survey metrics, which ultimately will drive improved business results. Both groups are interested parties in the gathering and assessing of future-state data. Together we review what the data uncovers and share accountability for improved results.

Success: In Chapter 7, the results I shared demonstrated success with each of the four teams that underwent HUM-B-LE development to date. While *we have not seen a case where outcomes haven't improved*, the LD professional's work is not complete until the improvement is verified. If the surveys show no statistical improvement, the LD professional would perform another round of data review with the Leadership team to understand what more needs to be done, then reengage with pertinent support. The work is not finished until employees' experience improvement.

Deliverable:

The final survey provides quantitative understanding of whether the objectives of the LD program have been met, and it creates Leader and LD professional accountability.

Chapter 15 Summary:

- Measuring the future state enables the LD program and the local Leaders to be accountable for enhancing engagement, improving psychological safety, which ultimately improves business results.
- Use of the HUM-B-LE development method consistently results in better survey scores.

Practice:

Consider the main improvement initiatives you are involved with. Have you identified how you will measure their success? Have the criteria been agreed to by all the accountable parties and has a meeting to review the success data been scheduled? If not, complete these activities.

CHAPTER 16

Wrapping it Up

I n Part 1, we dived deep into several areas vital to Leadership success:

- Humility
- Employee engagement
- Psychological safety
- Followership

I felt it worthwhile to devote time and attention to discussing how to grow strength in such powerful aspects of creating world-class teams.

I wrote this book with the intent to share a straightforward, practical approach for developing great Leaders. I hope you use it not only to elevate Leadership performance, but also to create winning teams that look forward to coming to work and unleashing their latent capabilities.

In Part 2, I've shared what I believe is a novel approach to a Leadership Development process, called HUMan-Based LEadership (HUM-B-LE) development. One that focuses on the LD Professional creating a partnership with individual

Leaders and their teams to deliver foundational, pertinent LD content. It's about getting to know your Leader(s)/customers and supporting them, starting where they are today. It's about engaging their team to share knowledge and build chemistry so they can learn, apply, and challenge each other to sustain LD concepts that have historically dissolved when the LD professional leaves.

This approach is also about laying a strong foundation of emotional intelligence that improves relationships, creates an openness to challenge, unleashes empowerment, and builds a basis for psychological safety. If you apply this approach in your team and in your organization, it will create improved team health, an increase in engagement, and a growth in followership for the Leaders.

The program outlined in this book highlights interpersonal skills required to be a great Leader. It glosses over the technical Leadership skills, under the assumption that training and development programs for these skills are documented elsewhere. The traditional LD topics are only as effective as *the ability of the team to productively apply them*, and application is what the HUM-B-LE approach enables.

It stands out in the ability to tap into the latent potential of all employees. Following the HUM-B-LE approach will unleash the limitless potential of employees, which is rarely achieved in organizations led by traditional leaders or managers. This approach grows great Leaders and teams.

Being good listeners, being humble, living in emotional intelligence—apply these and other skills in this book in every situation you go into. They signal personal growth, and they also highlight features that—studies show—can send your business soaring, with high employee retention. Try it. It works.

EPILOGUE/CONCLUSION

The genesis of this book came when I realized that across companies and within training and development approaches in professional organizations, LD methodologies seem to be artifacts of historic practice. But these approaches, as shown by contemporary research and surveys of industry, have limited value. And yet, in the last fifteen years impressive research has emerged, revealing insight into effective Leadership, learning science, and human dynamics. The dichotomy between common practice and twenty-first-century research on such topics as the importance of emotional intelligence and psychological safety demonstrated to me that our training and HR functions are behind the times. Moreover, there seemed to be a gap between the theoretical understanding of the role of Leaders and their daily, practical experiences.

Not only was I inspired to take a different approach when I became an LD professional, but I also had a strong desire to share my experiences with a larger audience. In short, my personal goal is to grow the effectiveness of the LD process in producing more capable Leaders. Growing better Leaders has a multiplier effect on individuals and society, creating more effective companies and healthier work environments. This is my mission, and I'm so grateful to be able to share it with you. May you use this to great value.

For more information, please visit **humessence.com**.

ACKNOWLEDGMENTS

I'm grateful to my wife, Kara Tate, for her encouragement, support, and constructive challenge. I would not have been able to write this book without her help. I'm also indebted to my teacher and mother, Lynn Larson, my work associate Gabe Campos, who was a partner in developing the HUM-B-LE approach, and my longtime friend and Leadership peer Karan Sangha for their review and wise counsel to improve this work. The support, advice, and encouragement I received from the people of the Self-Publishing School has also been invaluable in helping me get this project across the finish line. There are so many other people along the way who have helped, including friends supporting the book launch, all of whom have provided me feedback and challenged my paradigms. I am so very grateful for you all.

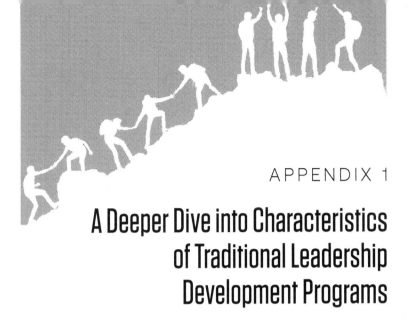

A Deeper Dive into Characteristics of Traditional Leadership Development Programs

L et's define what we mean by "traditional" Leadership Development programs. What characterizes them is how short lived the learning is. The traditional LD program takes place in a gathering of Leaders from across an organization who are at a similar level in their development. They come together to learn together, *not necessarily to implement the learning together.* This enables a company to "efficiently" deliver leadership concepts to the group. These programs require Leaders to leave their jobs to attend classes together as a cohort, receive the training over the course of several days, then return to their workplaces to implement what they've learned. This typically involves several of those "learn and apply" cycles, usually several weeks apart. When the last batch of classes is delivered, the program is complete. Leaders are now considered trained—expected to apply the concepts they've learned.

Often when, upon completion of this program, student satisfaction is measured, the quality of the training is measured. What these programs don't typically measure is the effectiveness by which these concepts are applied in the long term, nor the impact on business performance; neither do they typically measure culture improvement. This creates a disconnect between traditional programs and the desired effect on business results. One study, by Davd Coates (see Chapter 14) showed that at one-year post-program completion, only 34 percent of the Leaders reported they were still applying what they learned in the program. Yet, when a process for sustainment was added (in this study it was post-program coaching), the application of the learning two years after the conclusion of the class went up to 96 percent. Thus, sustainability is a key step not typically included in traditional LD programs. Other characteristics that I believe limit the effectiveness of the traditional approach include:

- Pushing a standard Leadership curriculum
- Emphasizing cohort versus coworker class attendance
- Promoting LD teachers without Leadership experience
- Ignoring relevance and timing
- Lacking ways to measure effectiveness
- Providing insufficient follow-up post-curriculum delivery

Pushing Leadership Curriculum

My personal Leadership-development experience has had more to do with organic feedback than coursework or formal

LD programs. As a Leader, my performance would periodically be reviewed and I'd receive feedback on what I was doing well, and where I could improve. Additionally, questionnaires filled in by my team would provide insight into its overall health and productivity. Over the course of these cycles, I would receive information specific to my approach and its impact on the team. Review and reflection with an HR partner or trusted mentor created the lion's share of my evolution because it was specific to what I needed.

This experience is indicative of a common human tendency to respond more effectively to directly relevant information, as opposed to generalized theory. Traditional LD programs push material on the student, with the philosophy that all curriculum is relevant for all students, and exposure to it will improve their personal effectiveness across the board. They are more focused on the efficient delivery of curriculum than on the application of concepts and their impact on the business. While there may be incremental value in this approach, it's far from being directly relevant or efficient in growing your specific abilities to Lead.

Contrast someone who comes in with the mindset of a partner, and who sits with the student Leader to review the survey data from the Leader's team. Together, they interpret the information and mine the data for insight. This personal identification of growth opportunities creates a pull from the Leader to evolve in personally relevant areas.

Cohort versus Coworker Classes

The traditional Leadership Development program consists of a group of Leaders or aspiring Leaders from all parts of an organization taking a course together. There is value in networking and growing relationships, but this comes at the expense of other attributes.

Invariably, individuals returning to their work environment are generally met with a barrage of work to catch up on that accumulated while they were in class. Even if they're willing and motivated to apply the new concepts, their individual and team capacity for learning and applying materials is challenged by busyness and time constraints. This limitation is generally not considered by the program, which instead assumes that sufficient capacity exists.

Cohort programs also mean that class attendees are generally a group disparate from all over an organization. This makes it more challenging to implement in local teams, who haven't had exposure to the training and who haven't scheduled in time to support implementation. I would argue that greater value is in effective implementation and not in networking.

LD Teachers without Leadership Experience

While terrific LD instructors exist who are very effective in their craft and may have developed a curriculum aligned with sound leadership theory, there's often a practical gap still between their knowledge and experience. Have they been Leaders tasked with creating an engaged team? In my experience, few of these instructors have the practical experience of their students. Without this, can they truly appreciate the nuanced application of the materials that Leaders face every day? Have they had to apply a concept to a whole range of personality types through times of calm and calamity? Have they had to adjust their approach on the run while dealing with an infinite variety of issues?

For these reasons, practical Leadership experience is an important asset for the instructor. This gap can be closed when the instructor engages with individual Leaders and teams, then partners with a Leader of the team to present information. This is an important attribute of the HUM-B-LE development method.

Relevance and Timing

A common characteristic of LD training is that it usually teaches generic material based on a broad, companywide assessment of needs. For example, the concept of creating an operating plan is a useful Leadership tool. However, if the local environment is toxic and there's no psychological safety, then there will be minimal participation in generating the plan. The plan can, for all intents and purposes, be irrelevant. Additionally, a student may learn how to create an operating plan in the August class, but not have the business need to apply it until the annual planning process in January.

The custom approach detailed in the HUM-B-LE development program enables the team to learn relevant concepts to address local opportunities and with a timing that aligns to application.

Lacking Effectiveness Measures

How do we know if the training that was delivered accomplished the intention of changing behaviors and making Leaders more effective? General assessments of these programs based on the quality of the training fall short of ensuring the development of more effective Leaders.

Sometime back, I was in a meeting where a decision was announced to discontinue one of these Leadership

Development cohort classes. I asked how the decision came about. "The program was costly and only served XX people last year" came the reply. My next question was, "Well, was the program effective? Did it create more effective Leaders? And were there positive business outcomes?" They had no idea because this traditional approach didn't measure the impact of the training on business objectives.

Yes, due to the significant time lag between the training and the measuring of the impact of improved Leadership, there are challenges with determining the size of LD program effects on business results. Additionally, this time lag introduces confounding factors that impact performance and create noise in the data. That said, such things as the effect of LD on the culture of the team is cleaner data and provides a better option for assessing LD value. Traditional LD programs don't typically measure these things, especially when classes are cohorts of disjointed Leaders.

Insufficient Follow-up Post-Curriculum Delivery

The best of traditional LD programs have instructors available for questions, and after the training is concluded, may schedule follow-up meetings. They may even set up concepts like "accountability buddies" to have peer Leaders support and coach each other post-training. But generally, traditional programs focus mainly on delivering content to the next cohort and tend to leave past cohorts behind. The long-term impact then becomes, as the rock group Kansas put it, "Dust in the Wind."

There are options in this area that create sustainment, as I've detailed in step 7 of the HUM-B-LE development method.

APPENDIX 2

Helpful Lists

Mindfulness Practices

Meditate

Journal

Set intentions at the start of each day

Make a list of what you're grateful for

Learn something new

Practice deep and present listening

Immerse in and observe nature

Go dancing

Learn or practice an instrument

Go on an adventure

Learn something new

L isten to a book, podcast, or Ted Talk and personally reflect on its meaning for you

Review the day for strong emotions, suboptimal actions, challenging interactions, etc. and, without judgment, assess them and reflect on what you can learn from them.

Energy Leadership Index—Attitude Levels. Where do you fall?

1. Victimized (I lose)
2. In Conflict/Defiant (You lose)
3. Take Responsibility (I win)
4. Concerned/In Service (You win)
5. Practice Reconciliation/Acceptance (We win, win/win)
6. Synthesize/Seek Wisdom (We always win)
7. Totally Nonjudgmental/In Flow (winning and losing are illusions/in the moment)

This model provides vocabulary to enable us to characterize our attitude. It enables us to be self-aware and to choose a higher level. And it enables peers to remind each other to be conscious of the attitude they're presenting.

Activities for Practicing DEI

- Engage in Diversity Mentoring: Identify interested employees from underrepresented groups (minorities, LGBTQ, disabled, etc.) and match them with a respected employee mentor.

- Do Reverse Mentoring: Each Leader asks someone from an underrepresented group to meet with them regularly to share their culture, perspective, ideas, frustrations, etc. The Leader will learn more than they could have imagined, and their world view will be greatly expanded.

- Study each of the steps in the process of identifying a need: creating a posting, marketing it, reviewing resumes and selecting candidates, choosing the interview team, holding the interview, deciding on a candidate, communicating the decision, and onboarding the new employee. Look for opportunities for subtle bias in each step of the process and take steps to remove it.

- Review diversity metrics, target biggest opportunities, and create projects for improvement. Share the data, the goals, and the projects. Monitor progress openly and include diversity groups in the conversation.

- In all opportunities act with inclusivity—toward both underrepresented groups and white males who may be feeling like the organization is overreaching. Don't shy away from these discussions or judge other perspectives. Create conversation and unite in getting educated on the issues together. Let the data do the talking.

LD Sustainment Ideas

- Form a Monthly Leadership book club
- Set up a Monthly discussion of E.I. topics with team members, rotating who suggests the topic.
- Organize a podcast or a TED Talk club.
- Create coaching "buddies."

- Schedule team or individual mindfulness sessions.
- Set up Roundtable meetings, with each person sharing one appreciation and one frustration.
- Add "Learn about someone's history" to the list of Leaders' routine work.
- Commit to hearing from everyone and in every meeting go around the room, giving everyone an opportunity to share.
- Have recognition time at the end of every weekly meeting.
- Have a ten-minute team walk outside at the end of lunch if time permits that day.
- Schedule feedback Fridays, where anyone can sign up to provide ten minutes of feedback.
- Schedule annual followership assessments.
- Role-play difficult conversations with peers before having the conversation.
- Teach E.I. to your team.
- Self-assess on tools like GlobeSmart and then discuss the results.
- Set up Self-reflection time at the end of each meeting: what was learned and what action should be taken?

QR Code for More Information on the HUM-B-LE program and LD Services Offered by Humessence, LLC

BIBLIOGRAPHY

Angelle, P. S. (2017). "Leading authentically: A new principal in challenging circumstances." *Research in Educational Administration & Leadership*, 2(1), 10–27.

Anseel, F., Leroy, H., Gardner, W. L., and Sels, L. (2015). "Authentic leadership, authentic followership, basic need satisfaction, and work role performance: A cross-level study." *Journal of Management*, 41(6), 1677–1697.

Apple TV. (2020). *Ted Lasso*.

Arets, J., Jennings, C., and Heijnen, V. "*702010 Towards 100% Performance.*" Sutler Media, 2016.

Bass, B. M. (1990). "From transactional to transformational leadership: Learning to share the vision." *Organizational Dynamics*, 18(3), 19–31.

Beer, M., Finnstrom, M., and Schrader, D. (Oct. 2016). "Why Leadership Training Fails—and What to Do About It." *Harvard Business Review*: 50–57.

Berger, J. B. (2014). "Leadership: A concise conceptual overview (Paper 18)." Amherst, MA: *Center for International Education Faculty Publications*.

Bower, M. (Nov. 1997). "Developing leaders in a business." *McKinsey Quarterly*.

Bradberry, T., Greaves, J. *Emotional Intelligence 2.0*. San Diego, CA: TalentSmart, 2009.

Brungardt, C. (2011). "The intersection between soft skill development and leadership education." *Journal of Leadership Education*, 10(1): 1–22.

Buckingham, M., and Clifton, D. *Now, Discover Your Strengths: The Revolutionary Program That Shows You How to Develop Your Unique Talents and Strengths—and Those of the People You Manage*. New York: The Free Press, A Division of Simon & Schuster Inc., 2001.

Buckingham, M., Coffman, C. *First, Break All the Rules: What the World's Greatest Managers Do Differently*. New York: Simon & Schuster, 1999.

Buckingham, M., Goodall, A. *Nine Lies about Work: A Freethinking Leader's Guide to the Real World*. Harvard Business Review Press, 2019.

Cavazotte, F., Moreno, V., and Hickmann, M. (2012). "Effects of leader intelligence, personality and emotional intelligence on transformational leadership and managerial performance." *The Leadership Quarterly*, 23(3): 443–455.

Coates, D. (2013). "Integrated leadership development programmes: Are they effective and what role does coaching play?" *International Journal of Evidence Based Coaching and Mentoring*, (S7): 39.

Collins, J. *Good to Great: Why Some Companies Make the Leap . . . and Others Don't.* HarperCollins Publishers, 2001.

Delizonna, L. (Aug. 24, 2017). "High-performing teams need psychological safety: Here's how to create It." *Harvard Business Review.*

Dyer, W. *Change Your Thoughts—Change Your Life: Living the Wisdom of the Tao.* Hay House, Inc., 2007.

Covey, S. R. *The Speed of Trust: The One Thing That Changes Everything.* New York: Free Press: a division of Simon and Schuster, 2006.

——. *The 7 Habits of Highly Effective People: Restoring the Character Ethic.* New York: A Fireside Book, Simon & Schuster, 1989.

DDI. "Global Leadership Forecast 2018." https://www. ddiworld.com/research/global-leadership-forecast-2018.

——. "CEO Leadership Report 2021." https://www.ddiworld. com/research/ceo-leadership-report.

Davey, L. *The Good Fight: Use Productive Conflict to Get Your Team and Organization Back on Track.* Publishers Group West, 2019.

Day, D. V. (2000). "Leadership development: a review in context." *Leadership Quarterly*, 11(4): 581.

de Vries, M. K., and Korotov, K. (2010). "Developing leaders and leadership development." *INSEAD Working Papers Collection* (77): 1–23.

Druskat, V. U., and Wolff, S. (March 2001). "Building the emotional intelligence of groups." *Harvard Business Review.* March: 78–90.

Duhigg, C. (Feb. 25, 2016). "What Google learned from its quest to build the perfect team." *The New York Times Magazine.* https://www.nytimes.com/2016/02/28/magazine/what-google-learned-from-its-quest-to-build-the-perfect-team.html.

Dust, S. B., Resick, C. J., Margolis, J. A., Mawritz, M. B., and Greenbaum, R. L. (2018). "Ethical leadership and employee success: Examining the roles of psychological empowerment and emotional exhaustion." *The Leadership Quarterly*, 29(5): 570–583.

Edmondson, A., (2019). *The Fearless Organization: Creating Psychological Safety in the Workplace for Learning, Innovation, and Growth.* John Wiley & Sons.

Engelbrecht, A. S., Heine, G., and Mahembe, B. (2014). "The influence of ethical leadership on trust and work engagement: An exploratory study." *SAJIP: South African Journal of Industrial Psychology*, 40(1): 1–9.

Eurich, T. (2018). (January 4, 2018). "What self-awareness really is (and how to cultivate it)". Hbr.org/2018/01/what-self-awareness-really-is-and-how-to-cultivate-it.

Frankl, V. *Man's Search for Meaning.* Beacon Press, 2006.

Gandossy, R., and Guarnieri, R. (2008). "Can you measure leadership?" *MIT Sloan Management Review*, 50(1): 65.

George, B. *Authentic Leadership: Rediscovering the Secrets to Creating Lasting Value.* Jossey-Bass, a Wiley imprint, 2003.

——. (Oct. 26, 2012). "Managing yourself: Mindfulness helps you become a better leader." *Harvard Business Review.*

GlobeSmart®. Aperian Global. https://www.globesmart.com/profile-culture-guides/.

Gushiken, K. M. (2019). "The softer side of leadership: Essential soft skills that transform leaders and the organizations they lead." *Christian Education Journal,* 16(1): 176–178.

Harvey, N. "Three lessons on leading through crisis from Barry Wehmiller." https://www.consciouscapitalism.org/story/three-lessons-on-leading-through-crisis-from-barry-wehmiller.

Hidden Brain, various episodes. https://hiddenbrain.org/category/podcast/page/21/.

Holt, S., Hall, A., and Gilley, A. (2018). "Essential components of leadership development programs." *Journal of Managerial Issues,* 30(2): 214–229.

Kernis, M. H., Goldman, M. B. (2006). "A multicomponent conceptualization of authenticity: Theory and research." *Advances in Experimental Social Psychology,* 38: 283–357.

Liedtka, J. (2008). "Strategy making and the search for authenticity." *Journal of Business Ethics,* 80(2): 237–248.

Leroy, H., Anseel, F., Gardner, W. L., and Sels, L. (2015). "Authentic leadership, authentic followership, basic need satisfaction, and work role performance: A cross-level study." *Journal of Management,* 41(6): 1677–1697.

Malik, S. H. (2012). "A study of relationship between leader behaviors and subordinate job expectancies: A path-goal approach." *Pakistan Journal of Commerce and Social Sciences* (2): 357. Retrieved from Merriam-Webster.

Misner, J. W. (2014). "Mindful leadership and navigating the seas of change in the information age." *Journal of Leadership Studies*, 8(2): 46–50.

Moldoveanu, M. Narayandas, D. (March–April 2019). "The future of leadership development." *Harvard Business Review*.

Northouse, P. G. (2016). *Leadership: Theory and Practice* (seventh edition). SAGE Publications, Inc.

Parris, D. L., Peachey, J. W. (2013). "A systematic literature review of servant leadership theory in organizational contexts." *J Bus Ethics*: 113:377–393. DOI 10.1007/s10551-012-1322-6.

Podsakoff, P. M., MacKenzie, S. B., Paine, J. B., and Bachrach, D. G. (2000). "Organizational citizenship behaviors: A critical review of the theoretical and empirical literature and suggestions for future research." *Journal of Management*, 26(3): 513–563.

Riggio, R. E. (2008). "Leadership development: The current state and future expectations." *Consulting Psychology Journal: Practice and Research*, 60(4): 383–392.

Rozovsky, J. (Nov. 17, 2015). "The five keys to a successful Google team." https://rework.withgoogle.com/blog/five-keys-to-a -successful-google-team/.

Ryan, R., Deci, E. *Self-determination Theory: Basic Psychological Needs in Motivation, Development, and Wellness.* The Guilford Press, 2018.

Sen, A. (2010). "Developing ambidextrous, connected and mindful brains for contemporary leadership." *International Journal of Business Insights & Transformation*, 3(2): 103–111.

Schneider, B. *Energy Leadership: Transforming Your Workplace and Your Life from the Core.* John Wiley & Sons, 2007.

Scullen, S. E., Mount, M. K., and Goff, M. (2000). "Understanding the latent structure of job performance ratings." *Journal of Applied Psychology*, 85(6): 956–970.

Sinek, S. *Start with Why: How Great Leaders Inspire Everyone to Take Action.* Penguin Audio, 2017.

Spreitzer, G. M. (2006). "Leading to grow and growing to lead: Leadership development lessons from positive organizational studies." *Organizational Dynamics*, 35(4): 305–315.

Sull, D., Sull, C. (Sept. 16, 2021). "10 Things your corporate culture needs to get right." *MIT Sloan Management Review.* https://sloanreview.mit.edu/article/10-things-your-corporate-culture-needs-to-get-right/.

Taylor, S. N. (2010). "Redefining leader self-awareness by integrating the second component of self-awareness." *Journal of Leadership Studies*, 3(4): 57–68.

Trinks, J. (2004). "Building great leaders at the IRS." *Industrial and Commercial Training*, vol. 36, no. 7: 262; *MIT Sloan Management Review*: 264.

Tripathi, P., Kohli, N. (2017). "Emotional intelligence as a predictor of employees general health." *Indian Journal of Health and Wellbeing*, 8(4): 263–267. http://www.iahrw.com/index.php/home/journal_detail/19#list.

Van Dierendonck, D., Stam, D., Boersma, P., De Windt, N., and Alkema, J. (2014). "Same difference? Exploring the differential mechanisms linking servant leadership and transformational leadership to follower outcomes." *The Leadership Quarterly*, 25(3): 544–562.

Whetstone, J. T. (2002). "Personalism and moral leadership: the servant leader with a transforming vision." *Business Ethics: A European Review*, 11(4): 385–392.

Wiseman, L. *Multipliers: How the Best Leaders Make Everyone Smarter*. Harper Business, an imprint of HarperCollins Publishers, 2017.

ABOUT THE AUTHOR

Brett Larson has been a Leader for more than thirty years, with the lion's share of his experience coming from Leadership roles in IMI Norgren and WL Gore and Associates. He received his BS in Industrial and Operations Engineering from the University of Michigan and MBA from the University of Colorado at Denver. He is also a Certified Professional Coach through the International Federation of Coaches (IFC), having received his training from the Institute of Professional Excellence in Coaching (iPEC). He has been a Leadership Development Program Manager since 2019, when he started researching and developing his unique approach in the field. He lives in Bend, Oregon with his wife, Kara, their dogs, Poe and Denali, and cats, Jeff and Smiles. He enjoys hiking, camping, biking, and supporting the local community.

Brett is a founding member of Humessence, LLC, an organization that implements HUM-B-LE within companies and delivers Leadership coaching. Our vision is to use this platform to help companies and individuals develop

Leadership greatness and grow high-performing teams. Great Leaders create engaged, rewarding environments of high-performance and personal satisfaction in all walks of life. His desire is to have a positive impact on the world, bringing consciousness and personal growth in both work and everyday life. Brett can be reached via Humessence.com and at brett@ humessence.com.

Request for Amazon Review

I would love to get your feedback on the book. How was its practicality? Clarity? Readability? How applicable is it to you at work or home? What would you like more information about? Feedback on all of these topics would be of huge value to me and future readers as I revise this text and help companies and Leaders grow their skills. Please share your thoughts in an Amazon review.

Made in the USA
Columbia, SC
10 March 2023

13590627R00096